AIR VANGUARD 5

ALBATROS D.I–D.II

JAMES F. MILLER

First published in Great Britain in 2012 by Osprey Publishing,
Midland House, West Way, Botley, Oxford, OX2 0PH, UK
43–01 21st St, Suite 220B, Long Island City, NY 11101, USA
E-mail: info@ospreypublishing.com

Osprey Publishing is part of the Osprey Group

A CIP catalog record for this book is available from the British Library

Print ISBN: 978 1 78096 599 4
PDF e-book ISBN: 978 1 78096 600 7
EPUB e-book ISBN: 978 1 78096 601 4

Index by Sharon Redmayne
Typeset in Deca Sans and Sabon
Originated by PDQ Digital Media Solutions Ltd., Suffolk, UK
Printed in China through Bookbuilders

13 14 15 16 17   10 9 8 7 6 5 4 3 2 1

www.ospreypublishing.com

Osprey Publishing is supporting the Woodland Trust, the UK's leading
woodland conservation charity, by funding the dedication of trees.

ACKNOWLEDGEMENTS

The author wishes to thank the following for their selfless contributions:

Jim, Major, and LaFonda Miller; Lance Bronnenkant; Chris and Charyn
Cordry; Tom and Karen Dillon; Jon Guttman; Jack Herris; Bert Hughlett;
Reinhard Kastner; Peter Kilduff; Herb and Sarah Kilmer; League of
World War One Historians; Koloman Mayrhofer; James G. and Judy
Miller; Naples Fitness Boot Camp; Marton Szigeti; Greg VanWyngarden;
Aaron Weaver; Reinhard Zankl.

CONTENTS

ALBATROS D.I–D.II

INTRODUCTION

When the Albatros D.I and D.II arrived in France during the late summer of 1916, only 13 years had elapsed since Ohio aviator Orville Wright flew his and his brother Wilbur's 12hp Wright Flyer on its 12-second, 120-foot inaugural flight. Powered aviation is now over a century old and the rate of development has slowed during its history. Technology and innovation progress inexorably, of course, but a Cessna 172 in 2013 is little different than one from 2000 – and, to a large degree, little different than one from 1970. Many of us have lived entire lives with seemingly omnipotent aeroplane types: the B-52 Stratofortress, A-10 Thunderbolt, F-15 Eagle, F-16 Fighting Falcon, Harrier, Boeing 747. Each has been in service over 30 years; the B-52 over 50 years. Little wonder that such longevity has caused many to overlook how new aviation really was in World War I, and yet how far it had progressed beyond the Wright Flyer.

Similarly, the progression of the Albatros D-series itself is noteworthy. The first D.Is at the Western Front in September 1916 were already accompanied by a D.II prototype. The D.II production machines that arrived in October were just two months ahead of the D.III, which entered service with a radically redesigned airfoil configuration developed via a prototype that had been designed and assembled prior to the arrival of the D.I! Four months hence, in April 1917, a licence-built variant of the D.III was ordered into production, along with the new Albatros D.V (the D.IV was a platform for geared engine tests and never produced as a front-line fighter), which featured a redesigned fuselage cross-section and rerouted aileron control cables from the lower to the upper wings. The first D.Vs reached the Front in May 1917, only three months before the first production order was placed for the last series of Albatros fighters, the D.Va. Meanwhile, licence-built Austro-Hungarian D.IIs entered service in May 1917, shortly followed in June by the Austro-Hungarian D.III, which was eventually redesigned with a rounded nose that eliminated the need for a spinner. Therefore, within its first year the Albatros D featured these six different models (11 when including all the

These Jasta 6 machines illustrate the three major redesigns of the pre-sesquiplane Albatros Ds. (R-L): D.I with inverted 'V' centre section struts; D.II with lowered upper wing and 'N' centre section struts; and a D.II with an engine radiator in the upper wing.

licence-built variants) that employed four major redesigns and had a total operational lifespan of 25 months – a design, production, and service rapidity that is unheard of today. Even so, 25 months was roughly half of World War I, an impressive service life for an aeroplane involved in that conflict.

Although little more than a decade removed from the era when aeroplanes resembled a jumbled assembly of fabric-covered ladders, the Albatros D.I design was already sleek and aware of aerodynamic efficiency, exemplified by a smooth fuselage, streamlined struts to reduce parasitic drag, and wing root fairings to reduce interference drag. Aside from landing and flying wires needed to help support the wings, most of the machine's aerodynamic detriments were actually cooling attributes: the machine guns, exposed engine-cylinder water jackets, and fuselage-mounted Windhoff radiators all employed the cooling effects of the passing airstream. The machines enjoyed excellent overall construction qualities, and, although their successors would be hampered by serious structural weakness when redesigned into a sesquiplane, when the D.I and D.II arrived in France they were the cream of any nation's fighter crop. Well built, sleek, rugged, fast, heavily armed, and easy to fly, in the latter months of 1916 the skies of France were theirs for the taking.

Regarding the impact of Albatros's new fighters, Royal Flying Corps pilot 2Lt Edmund Llewelyn Lewis, flying DH.2s with 32 Sqn, wrote:

> It rather feeds you up to see all this newspaper talk about our supremacy in the air. We certainly had it last June, July and August, but we haven't got it now. The Huns [slang for Germans, and also German aeroplanes] still keep to their side of the line while we venture over their lines, but if they wished they could sit over our aerodrome (with their fast machines) and we could do nothing against them. What I mean is that a DH [2] is no longer attacking, but is fighting for its life against these fast Huns, and that at present we have only about half-a-dozen machines to cope with them. But I suppose war in the air will always be like that. First one side has the best machines and then the other, and the side which shows most guts all through will be the winners. During this war, first we had the lead with the BEs and Vickers, then the Germans got it with the Fokkers. After that we got it with the DHs, and now the Huns are a bit superior with their fast scouts [Albatros D.I and D.II].

DESIGN AND DEVELOPMENT

After France and England stopped Germany's invasion of France before it reached Paris, both sides built elaborate systems of defensive trenches that spanned from the North Sea to the border of neutral Switzerland. Offensive mobility gave way to the static trench warfare of 'No Man's Land' and, by 1915, the war that was expected to be over by Christmas was deadlocked with no end in sight. By the end of 1915, 1,292,000 French, 612,000 German, and 279,000 British soldiers had been killed or wounded (these figures are approximate; casualty figures vary) in ground campaigns that resulted in little to no territorial advancement.

During this series of campaigns, aeroplanes played an important yet initially less lethal role, conducting the reconnaissance crucial for armies to formulate strategy. While tethered observation balloons had performed this service along both sides of the Front, aerial observation via mobile photo-reconnaissance aeroplanes saw an increasing role that proved valuable by providing real-time views of enemy forces that would have been unattainable otherwise. Initially these observation aeroplanes – two-seater machines with a pilot and dedicated observer – flew about unmolested save for anti-aircraft fire, but increasing encounters with their enemy counterparts inspired crews to take aloft rifles to exchange potshots. The value of attaining an aerial reconnaissance advantage over one's enemy while denying him the same was so clear that eventually both sides sought the use of quick, single-seat 'scouts' – originally developed to use speed to dash across the lines, conduct a visual tactical observation, and then race back to report the findings – for two-seater reconnaissance aeroplane interdiction and destruction.

Initially these single-seaters were hamstrung by the problem of synchronizing a forward-firing machine gun to shoot through a spinning propeller arc: it could not be done. French and German efforts to synchronize machine-gun fire had begun in 1910, although they involved little to no military support and were hampered by hang fires that disrupted the required steady gunfire cadence. By 1914 the French aeroplane manufacturer Morane-Saulnier had developed a synchronizer gear, but ground gunnery tests revealed hang fires, and the irregular firing rate of the open-bolt light machine guns being used still caused some bullets to strike the propeller. While sorting out these teething troubles, Raymond Saulnier devised a back-up solution of installing steel wedges to the propeller that deflected the bullets that would otherwise have shattered the wooden blades. These wedges underwent several successful tests until apparently one detached in flight, causing a significant imbalance that required a dead-stick forced landing. Further tests were delayed to repair the aeroplane and redesign the propeller to mount the deflector wedges better, but in early 1915 French pilot Sgt Roland Garros, who as a civilian had conducted some of the pre-war test flights in 1914, proposed trying the device again in action – and with his aeroplane so equipped shot down three German machines in two weeks. Unfortunately, on 18 April, engine failure (which some believe was caused by ground fire) led to Garros' forced landing and the capture of the device, which was delivered to Doberitz for evaluation by Idflieg (Inspektion der Fliegertruppen, or Inspectorate of Flying Troops) with the expectation of improving it for use on German machines.

One man contacted for this was Dutchman Anthony Fokker. Born on 6 April 1890 in Bliter, Java (modern Indonesia), Fokker's affluent family lived on their Java coffee plantation until returning to the Netherlands in 1894 to begin their children's formal education. Anthony proved to be a lacklustre student, yet developed an interest and aptitude for independently studied mechanical subjects, such as woodworking, electricity, and steam-engine construction. Fokker left school in 1908 and, after a brief military stint, formed a partnership with Oblt von Daum, an ex-military officer, to build aeroplanes. In 1911 he used one to teach himself how to fly and soon acquired a reputation as an 'amazingly sure' pilot. After various aeroplane builds and trials funded by his father, Fokker received his first aeroplane order from the German army, which led to further orders and the establishment of his own company along Ostorfer Lake in Schwerin-Gorries, Mecklenburg.

In 1913 Fokker acquired a Morane-Saulnier Type H, a machine that formed the basis for his future designs and created the lineage of famous monoplanes, the Fokker E-types. When war began the following year, Fokker enjoyed increased German military production orders but he did not yet possess adequate facilities to fulfil them. Upon realizing this, Idflieg advised him to expand his facilities, abandon his work on new types, and concentrate on production rather than innovation. After all, the war was expected to be over by Christmas. Innovation was for the future; Germany needed arms *now*.

However, when Garros' machine fell into German hands, the timing was perfect for Fokker. For months his company had been experimenting with a means by which a fixed machine gun could be fired through a propeller arc via an interrupter gear (believed to have been based on a 1913 patent held by Franz Schneider, a Swiss with the German firm Luftverkehrsgesellschaft [LVG]), which prevented the weapon from firing whenever a propeller blade passed before the muzzle. This was the best solution to enable forward firing gunnery for tractor-powered aeroplanes, but came at a price: interrupter linkages were sensitive to temperature changes and wear, required vigilant preventative and/or reparative maintenance, and synchronization negatively affected the rate of fire because of variable propeller rpms. For example, Fokker's system allowed the gun to fire once for each propeller revolution. A rate of fire set at 500 rounds per minute would be supported up to propeller speeds of 500rpm. When the propeller exceeded 500rpm, the interrupter could not keep up and thus only permitted firing on every other rotation, cutting the rate of fire in half. Although the increase in rate of fire was still commensurate with increased propeller rpms, it was now at half the rate. When the engine rpms reached 1,000 the rate of fire returned again to 500 because the interrupter could not keep up, and now the gun had to fire every third propeller rotation, or 330 rounds per minute. An attacking pilot could make a reduced-power descent via a blip-switch and experience several different rates of fire as engine rpms waxed and waned from the blipping. Therefore, all noted synchronized machine gun rates of fire are maximum rates, not constant.

Fokker demonstrated his interrupter gear at Doberitz a month after the capture of Garros' aeroplane and was awarded a production contract for aeroplanes so equipped. As German Fliegertruppe Commander General Ernst von Hoeppner wrote in post-war memoirs,

> The true Kampfflugzeug [combat airplane] originated first with the utilization of the invention of Fokker, which made it possible to fire through the propeller arc. The fixed machine-gun was now operated by the pilot himself. The omission of the observer produced in this new E-type aeroplane extraordinary speed, manoeuvrability and climbing ability.

This new E-type was the Fokker Eindecker I, a mid-wing monoplane powered by an air-cooled rotary engine of 80Ps (a measure of horsepower [*Pferedestärke*, or Ps], where 1.0hp equals 1.014Ps) rotary engine. By mid-1915, German pilots used this new weapon to attack enemy reconnaissance aeroplanes and created a desperate period for the Allies during which Germany held tactical air superiority. Initially the Allies had no effective machine with which to counter this threat and necessarily changed their tactics to state that

A Morane-Saulnier Type N with propeller-mounted bullet deflector wedges. Although many believe these wedges to have been simple triangular blocks of steel from which bullets ricocheted, in actuality they featured furrowed channels designed purposely to direct a bullet away from the blades.

Fokker's rotary-engined E I, equipped with a single Parabellum LMG 14 machine gun synchronized to fire through the propeller arc, was considered by Fliegertruppe commander General Ernst von Hoeppner to be Germany's 'first true Kampfflugzeug'. This particular machine was flown by FFA 6b's Ltn Kurt Wintgens in summer 1915.

'a machine proceeding on reconnaissance must be escorted by at least three other fighting machines ... and a reconnaissance should not be continued if any machines become detached.' Four aeroplanes were now required to do the work of one.

Meanwhile, as the horror of Verdun continued through 1916, the French urged a British offensive to lessen France's military burden. Towards that end, the British launched the Battle of the Somme on 1 July. But by then the 'Fokker Scourge' had been countered by the arrival of Allied single-seat biplane fighters, namely French Nieuports, and as the British and German armies slogged through yet another bloodbath – British casualties on the first day alone of the battle of the Somme were some 19,000 killed and 41,000 wounded – British F.E.2 and DH.2 biplane pushers joined the French Nieuport in dominating the skies, enjoying complete superiority that they maintained throughout the summer.

Fokker attempted to alter this situation by increasing the power of his monoplanes with twin-row rotary engines and augmenting firepower with two and sometimes three machine guns (as seen with the Fokker E IV), but these changes hamstrung performance to the point of pilot dissatisfaction. 'In

 ALBATROS D.I 390/16 OF LTN D R OTTO HÖHNE, JAGDSTAFFEL 2, SEPTEMBER 1916

One of several pre-production D.Is acquired by Jasta 2, 390/16 is depicted in pristine factory condition, save for the first two letters of the pilot's last name that were painted on the fuselage. Opinions differ regarding whether the fuselage remained unpainted 'straw yellow' birch or if it was stained/overpainted a darker color, as seen in a photograph of this machine taking off, but since the specific film type is unknown it is difficult to determine how much the photographic values have been altered. What is clear is that if overpainted, the vents, cowls, and access hatches were not, and in any case the dark wing root fairings suggest they were wood and not metal. Wings and horizontal stabilizer surfaces are shown in two-tone venetian red/olive green camouflage, the exact pattern of which is provisional, and the rudder is depicted overpainted in the 'swirl' pattern seen on several pre-production Albatros Ds. Höhne achieved six victories with Jasta 2 but was wounded in action on 10 January 1917. After convalescing he assumed command of Jasta 59 in December but on 26 January 1918 returned to Jasta 2 as Staffelführer, only to voluntarily relinquish his command in less than a month on the grounds he was 'not mature enough for the requirements.

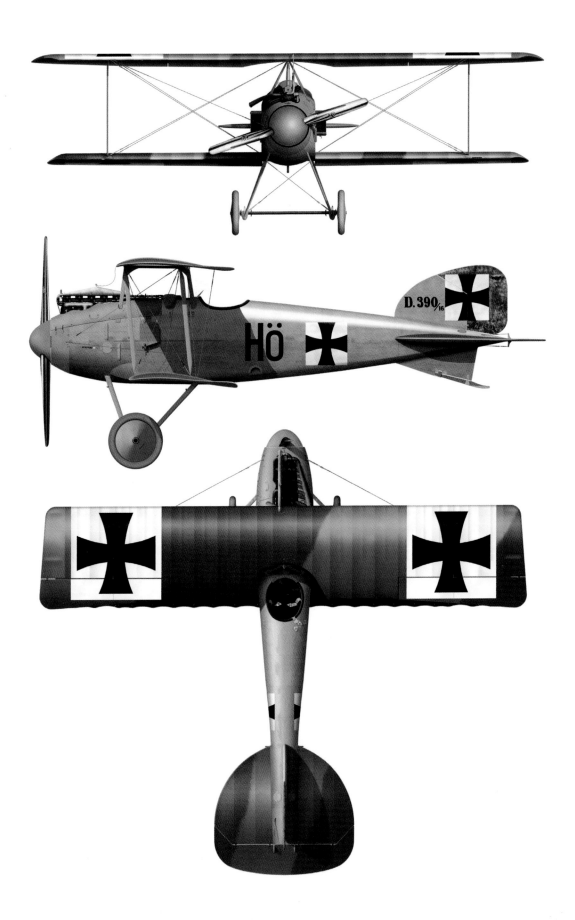

a climb,' reported Germany's leading ace and Orden Pour le Mérite-decorated Hptm Oswald Boelcke, '[the E IV] loses speed to such an extent that Nieuport biplanes have repeatedly escaped me.' This helped foster a sea change amongst the Fliegertruppe that future German machines ought to be of biplane rather than monoplane construction. Future 44-victory ace and Orden Pour le Mérite winner Obltn Rudolf Berthold opined

we had fallen asleep on the laurel wreaths that the single-seaters in the hands of a few superlative pilots [Boelcke, Immelmann, Wintgens] had achieved. It was not the monoplane itself, but the pilots who were responsible for the success.

In early 1916 several aeroplane manufacturers began designing single-seat fighters that utilized in-line water-cooled engines, rather than the air-cooled rotary engines that powered the Fokker E-types. One such manufacturer was Halberstädter Flugzeugwerke GmbH. This was an ambitious move for Halberstadt, who previously had built two-seater trainers for their flight school. Their D.I prototype flew in late autumn 1915, powered by a 100Ps Mercedes D.I engine. Their next prototype was designated D.III, powered by a 120Ps Argus engine. This particular machine reached the Front in February 1916, presumably outside the normal distribution channels, and is theorized to have been a 'presentation gift'.

In March 1916 Halberstadt received a letter of intent authorizing the construction of 12 of their D.Is and D.IIs; the low production figure suggests Idflieg's caution with the company's inexperience. The letter specified that these machines should carry a 150kg (330lb) useful load that included one synchronized machine gun with 500 rounds of ammunition; a maximum speed of 145km/h (90mph); and the ability to climb to 4,000m (13,124 feet) in 40 minutes (an average of 100m or 325ft per minute). These requirements were exceeded when the first production aeroplanes were flown in May.

The Halberstadt D.II was a sleek and somewhat spindly-looking machine. The fuselage was wood-framed, wire-braced, and covered in three-ply wood from the nose to aft of the cockpit, where doped-fabric-covered stringers sloped aft to seam the rounded forward fuselage with the slab-sided rear portion. The engine compartment was enclosed by detachable metal panels through which water-jacketed engine cylinders protruded, aft of which a single synchronized machine gun was fitted to starboard. Doors and hatches positioned on the three-ply permitted quick engine access, and a spring-loaded footstep was positioned on the lower port longeron adjacent to the three-ply–fabric transition. The wood-framed, twin-spar wings were of rectangular planform with slightly raked tips, internally wire-braced, and skinned with doped fabric. Ailerons were attached only to the outboard trailing edges of the upper wings. Their control cables were externally routed down to and through the lower wings, which were attached to the bottom fuselage longeron. The upper wings were attached to a cabane section that housed a gravity-fed fuel tank and airfoil radiator, and the upper and lower wings were attached to each other via twin sets of wire-braced streamlined steel

The single-gunned Halberstadt D.II was at the forefront of Germany's focus on in-line engine, biplane fighters. Although its performance was praised beyond that of the Fokker Eindecker, there remained calls for aeroplanes with increased engine power and a second machine gun.

tube struts; i.e. a two-bay design. Stagger was well forward, with the upper wing close to the fuselage. The empennage consisted of steel tube-framed and fabric-covered stabilators and a somewhat triangular steel tube-framed 'all-flying' rudder supported by streamlined steel tube 'inverted V' struts that connected the rudder post with the port and starboard longerons. Landing gear was of orthodox V-strut configuration, with streamlined steel tube struts supporting 28-inch wheels and a tubular steel axle. The wooden tailskid was fitted with a metal shoe, bungeed for a measure of shock absorption, and was supported by a tabular steel tripod.

Fokker, possessing greater experience with single-seater types, albeit of monoplane configuration, was awarded an 80-machine contract for his single-seat biplane fighter, the Fokker D.I. The Fokker D.I began life in June 1916 as prototype M 18, a single-bay single-seater with the wing gap filled by the fuselage in the same manner as the LFG Roland C.II Walfisch. The machine was powered by an in-line, water-cooled, 100Ps Mercedes D.I engine. Using a water-cooled engine was radically different from his usual use of rotary engines; Fokker claimed that 'the adaptation of the water-cooled engine for use in fighting planes by air headquarters came about through my efforts.' Engine cooling was provided by thin, flat radiators fitted to the port and starboard fuselages between wings that were attached to the upper and lower longerons, leaving a square area atop the fuselage through which the pilot's head and shoulders protruded. The wings did not have ailerons and instead

Anthony Fokker standing next to his two-bay 'M.18,' the Fokker D.I prototype. Note the 120Ps Mercedes D.II engine, Windhoff fuselage radiator, jewelled cowl panels, and the rectangular 'all flying' rudder that was replaced by the classic 'comma' shaped rudder on production machines.

were warped by the pilot to control roll: the outer wings were moved or 'warped' by control cables into different shapes that altered the way they met the relative wind, changing lift. Armament was a single synchronized forward-firing, air-cooled Maxim lMG 08.

Unfortunately, climb performance did not meet expectations, and by March the prototype had undergone several alterations. These included using a 120Ps Mercedes engine; replacing the single-bay design with one of two bays; creating a slimmer fuselage that used an open cabane structure that increased visibility from the cockpit; balanced ailerons replacing wing-warping for control of roll (although the production models reverted back to warping); and the rectangular radiators being replaced by boxier radiators made by Windhoff. The empennage employed horizontal stabilators and a similarly shaped 'all flying' tail; there were no elevators or rudder control surfaces. Armament remained the single Maxim.

In June 1916, the 120Ps Halberstadt D.II was the first German biplane single-seat fighter to reach the Front. Its superior qualities over the monoplane were noted in an Idflieg report that July:

> The Halberstadt with the 120Ps Mercedes engine has flown at the Front with good results and is well regarded; especially praised are its ability to climb and manoeuvre. It is decidedly preferred to the 160Ps [rotary engine] Fokker [E IV]. However, everyone urgently requests twin machine guns but this will lead to a corresponding reduction in performance.

June 1916 was also the month that Albatros Flugzeugwerke GmbH – known before solely for production of two-seater machines during the war – was awarded a contract for 12 single-seat biplane fighters. Albatros's history harkens back to the development of German aviation, when during much of the first decade of the 20th century Germany's aviation aspirations focused on lighter rather than heavier-than-air flight. Having formed a Luftschiffer Detachement (Lighter-than-air Detail) in 1884 to evaluate the reconnaissance applications of balloons, by 1901 the Detachement had grown into a Luftschiffer Batallion (Lighter-than-air Battalion) that employed free and moored balloons. In 1900 the first practical powered flight of a lighter-than-air machine occurred via a 17-minute flight of Graf Zeppelin's rigid airship LZ 1, and this event piqued Kriegsministerium (War Ministry) interest in the craft's possible military usefulness. Still, new heavier-than-air machines were not unknown. In 1905 the Americans Orville and Wilbur Wright brought their aeroplane to Europe to demonstrate controlled powered flight, and illustrated its practicality in a flight of 39km. Yet the War Ministry conference of 1906 established that German military aeronautics ought to focus on rigid airships, in large part due to their familiarity with lighter-than-air machines versus the newer heavier-than-air machines.

1909 saw a boom in the interest and development of the aeroplane. Public money was used to promote aeroplane development, demonstration flights were conducted, and the first German flight meeting took place at the inaugural German aerodrome at Johannisthal, near Berlin. Various manufacturers came to Johannisthal and under licence began building aeroplanes of foreign design, but in October a 3km flight at Johannisthal netted the pilot a 40,000-mark prize for the first flight of a German aeroplane powered by a German aero engine. Lighter-than-air machines still retained the focus of the German military, but many people realized that the aeroplane was coming of age.

One such person was German biologist Dr Walther Huth. Born in Altenburg in 1875, Huth was the son of a Prussian major and for 13 years had followed his family's traditional military calling before leaving the service in 1908 to study natural sciences. After meeting French aviation pioneer Hubert Latham, Huth so embraced the thought of flight via aeroplane that he sent his chauffeur Simon Brunnhuber to France and paid for his flight training there. Upon its successful completion, Brunnhuber returned with a Levasseur Antoinette single-seat monoplane that Huth had purchased; later he also bought a Farman two-seater. Huth, recognizing the aeroplane's importance for future military applications, contacted the Kriegsministerium in October 1909 and offered the services of his aeroplanes for flight instruction *gratis*, with Brunnhuber serving as instructor. While the subsequent negotiations were under way, Huth established his own company at Johannisthal that December, the Albatros Flugzeugwerke GmbH, named after the seabird with which he was familiar from his scientific studies.

Negotiations with the Militärbehörde (Military Authority) lasted until March 1910, when they accepted Huth's proposal. It is believed flight instruction began that July, and by March 1911 Brunnhuber had trained six pilots. Progress had been slow due to lack of funds, suitable training space (aeroplane engines frightened the horses of troops training nearby), and lingering doubts regarding the aeroplane's useful military role; there were also concerns about long training times for aeroplane maintenance personnel. Regardless, training continued as Albatros was contracted to build lattice-framed Farman reproductions with the type designation Albatros MZ 2.

In 1912 Albatros hired Diplom-Ingenieur (engineering graduate) Robert Thelen as chief designer. Born in Nürnberg on 23 March 1884, Thelen had studied mechanical engineering at the Royal Technical College of Charlottenburg in Berlin, graduating in 1909. A year later Thelen was the ninth German pilot trained (FAI [Fédération Aeronautique Internationale]-Brevet 9, from 11 May 1910) and became a competition pilot flying Wright biplanes. He then teamed up with Dipl-Ing Helmut Hirth (FAI-Brevet 79 from 11 March 1911). Employing the perfected semi-monocoque wooden fuselage designs of Ober-Ingenieur Hugo Grohmann (using a construction technique that provided enough strength via the external skin to eliminate the need for

Albatros chief designer Diplom-Ingenieur Robert Thelen chats from the cockpit of an Albatros-Doppeldecker. Note the wood-skinned fuselage, a future Albatros hallmark. A mechanical engineering graduate, Thelen was a licensed pilot and had flown Wright biplanes in competition prior to joining Albatros in 1912. (Photo courtesy of DEHLA Collection)

internal bracing, thereby reducing weight and increasing performance and payload capacity), Thelen's designs moved away from the Farman-type open-lattice construction as Albatros began building newly designed aeroplanes with the type of enclosed wooden fuselages (Rumpf-Doppeldecker, or fuselage double-decker [biplane]) for which they would become renowned. Chief among these would be the Albatros Type DD, later known as the B I, designed in early 1913 by Ernst Heinkel (whose future company produced many aeroplanes in World War II) and improved by Thelen's suggestions based on his experience as a pilot; Thelen referred to the type as 'Albatros DD, system Heinkel-Thelen'. Powered by a 100Ps Mercedes D.I engine, the semi-monocoque three-bay (Dreistielig) DD was a successful design that set several world records for duration and altitude in the months prior to World War I. That summer, a single-bay version known as the Renndoppeldecker powered by a 100Ps Hiero engine won the 100km speed prize at the Aspern Flugmeeting in Vienna, Austria. Experience gained with this machine is considered to have sown the seeds for the future Albatros D.I.

After World War I broke out in August 1914, Albatros concentrated on manufacturing two-seat B- and C-type machines. Aerial observation and artillery spotting were crucial for the support of ground forces and required that these machine types had manufacturing and engine allocation priority. As the war progressed, the opposing forces developed single-seat fighters to protect their two-seater observation machines and destroy those of the enemy, but mostly these fighters had been powered by rotary engines; those powered by in-line engines had been somewhat hamstrung by a lack of available higher horsepower engines, which were prioritized for the B- and C-type machines. This affected the early Fokker and Halberstadt D-types that employed 100 or 120Ps engines rather than engines of 160Ps, although Fokker later claimed to be the victim of a conspiracy to deny him use of a 160Ps engine. In any event, engine availability did not lessen the calls from fighter pilots requesting single-engine machines be equipped with higher-horsepower engines and armed with two rather than the then-standard single machine gun. German pilots also thought that while rotary engine fighters, with their rapid capacity for engine start and take-off, were ideal for intercepting enemy machines, a fighter powered by the more reliable in-line engine and armed with twin machine guns would be better suited to protect two-seater aeroplanes beyond enemy lines. Although German aerial tactics evolved differently, this mindset came at a time of increasing engine manufacturing productivity and set the stage for the birth of a new breed of fighter.

And none too soon. Tactical German aerial domination, once held by rotary-engined Fokker and Pfalz E-type wing-warping monoplanes, had been lost to the more nimble French Nieuport and British DH.2s, which not only outflew the German fighters but were also present in greater numbers. Rather than compete with the manoeuvrability of these

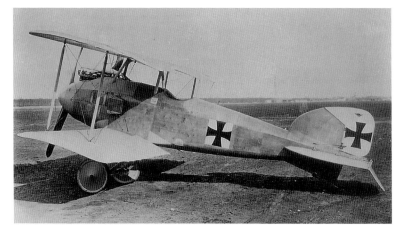

Albatros D.I prototype at Johannisthal. Note the clear-doped-linen wings, tail, and no windscreen. Noteworthy items changed prior to production include the upturned exhaust manifold, unbalanced elevator, externally routed rudder cables, and Eisernkreuz located on the rudder only—although this last would be a markings feature on Oeffag-built Albatrosses.

adversaries, the Thelen-led Albatros design bureau set to work on what became the Albatros D.I and D.II. By April 1916, the bureau had developed a sleek yet rugged machine that featured the usual Albatros semi-monocoque wooden construction and employed a 160Ps Mercedes D.III engine. Visual hallmarks of the D.I and early production D.II include fuselage-mounted Windhoff radiators and matching chords for the upper and lower wings.

Prior to its use with the Albatros D.I, the Mercedes D.III engine had powered aloft many two-seater reconnaissance aeroplanes that outweighed the D.I. Employing the same engine in the much lighter single-seat scout seemed obvious as regards the performance benefits to be reaped, and it was more than enough to carry aloft two machine guns and 1,000 rounds of ammunition and still have power available to provide speed, climb, and height beyond that of two-seaters. For example, the Mercedes D.III gave the 1,353kg (2,983lb fully loaded) Albatros C.III a maximum speed of 140 km/h (87mph) and a 45-minute average climb to 3,000m (9,843ft). The same engine in the 898kg (1,980lbs) Albatros D.I – some 453kg (1,003lbs) lighter than the Albatros C.III – gave the new single-seater a maximum speed of 175km/h (109mph) and a 19-minute climb to 3,000m.

On 6 June 1916 an Albatros D.I prototype began flight evaluation and static-load testing at the Adlershof test centre. Results were mixed. A test flight yielded a climb rate of 1,000m in 4 minutes, 2,000m in 8 minutes, 3,000m in 14 minutes, and 4,000m in 22 minutes; good results even when considering the machine was unarmed and thus lighter than gross weight. Yet in static-load tests the D.I's rear upper wing spar failed the load requirements for pulling out of a dive, and when retested on 3 July, it failed again. Tests for gliding flight and inverted flight requirements were passed on 4 and 5 July, and two days later a new wing spar was tested, which finally passed as well. Meanwhile, Idflieg had ordered 12

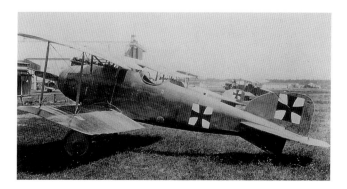

Port-forward view of the pre-production Albatros D.II 386/16. Note the outwardly splayed N-struts, centrally-located wing radiator, and the prominent above-wing header tank that is taller than the one seen later that autumn. The propeller is an Axial, and it displays that company's early 'dagger' style logo.

pre-production machines (D.380/16–391/16), of which several were armed and eventually sent forward for combat evaluation. By July the Zentral Abnahme Kommision (ZAK, or Central Acceptance Commission) recommended the Albatros D.I for production, after which Idflieg signed an order for 100 Albatros fighters. Fokker, too, received a production order for 40 Fokker D.IVs but Idflieg had expressed concerns regarding workmanship: 'The [Fokker D.I] makes an impeccable impression from 20 metres but with respect to quality of workmanship and the nature of technical details, it is recommended that Herr Fokker emulate the Albatros D.I.' Indeed, poor workmanship would plague the Fokker company several times throughout the war.

Concurrent with the development of the Albatros D.I, Thelen's team had designed and constructed a second, similar machine, the Albatros D.II. It is important to note that the Albatros D.I and D.II evolved simultaneously, and that development of the D.II was not the result of post-combat feedback from D.I pilots. Proof is found not only in photographs but in the pre-production order of 12 machines, of which one was D.II 386/16 (which became Oswald

ALBATROS D.II 501/16, JAGDSTAFFEL 2, LATE 1916/EARLY 1917

This first production batch D.II is depicted in standard factory appearance, with an unpainted birch fuselage and three-tone olive green/venetian red/pale green wing and stabilizer camouflage. Lighter areas suggest repairs using unpainted fabric. Known to have been flown by Oblt Adolf von Tutschek in early 1917, researcher Reinhard Kastner reveals 501/16 may have been a 'hand-me-down' from Manfred von Richthofen after his departure for Jasta 11. On the reverse of a photograph depicting this machine next to an observation balloon nest, handwritten details claim the pilot had been Richthofen, who after an engine failure of unknown causes was forced to make an emergency landing. The accuracy of this description is unverified, and generally Richthofen is associated with flying D.II 481/16 while serving with Jasta 2, but certainly it was common for pilots to fly various machines due to repairs and routine maintenance. Whatever the ownership, Richthofen and Tutschek went on to command Jagdgeschwader Nrs 1 and 2 respectively, were both wounded in the summer of 1917, and were ultimately killed in action within five weeks of each other while flying Fokker Triplanes in March and April, 1918.

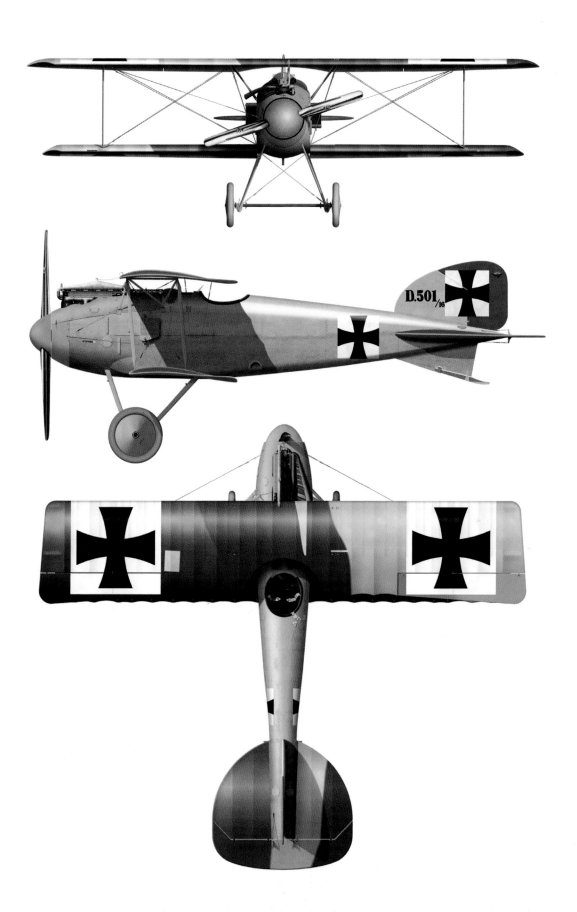

An Albatros D.II(OAW) serving with Jagdstaffel 14. Identifying OAW features include creased engine cowl edges, large forward wing root fairing, manufacturer and Idflieg placards near the cockpit, covered longeron seam (dark on this machine), and forward fuselage Eisernkreuz. Obscured is the port-plumbed radiator pipe, visible in other photos of this machine.

Sixteen Albatros D.IIs were built by the Austrian Aircraft Factory (Oesterreichische Flugzeugfabrik AG, or Oeffag) and the first, 53.01, is seen here. Differences from German D.IIs include the Daimler Dm 185 engine (its enclosing cowl removed in this photograph); engine-turned 'swirls' on the bare metal panels, hatches and wing root fairings; and the thick cross well forward.

Boelcke's machine) and one (D.388/16) was a prototype Albatros D.III. Essentially the D.I and D.II were the same machine with several noticeable external differences and improvements. The D.I's inverted V-strut centre section pylon had been replaced by outwardly splayed N-struts, which allowed the upper wing to be lowered 9.8 inches (250mm) to improve upward visibility without restricting forward visibility from the converging inverted V-struts at head-level. The side-mounted Windhoff radiators were replaced with a Teeves and Braun wing-mounted radiator located between the new N-struts. The latter modification did not take effect until after the first production run of 50 D.IIs (excluding Boelcke's pre-production D.II 386/16, built with a wing-mounted radiator), which made up the second half of Idflieg's first order for 100 Albatros fighters (50 D.Is, 422–471/16; 50 D.IIs, 472–521/16).

In August 1916, 50 more D.IIs (890–939/16) were ordered from Huth's Ostdeutsche Albatros Werke (at the time an independent firm that would be

assimilated into the main Albatros company in October 1917), located in Schneidmühl. These machines were designated Albatros D.II (OAW) and constructed almost identically to those built at Johannisthal, as were the 75 machines (1024–1098/16) built under license by LVG (Luftverkehrsgesellschaft), also ordered in August 1916. September saw Albatros receive the final D.II production order for 100 machines (1700–1799/16), after which production focus shifted to the next generation of Albatros fighters, the D.III (see Osprey's Duel 36 *SPAD VII vs Albatros D III*).

In December the Oesterreichische Flugzeugfabrik AG (Austrian Aircraft Factory, or Oeffag) received a production order for 20 Albatros D.IIs for use with the Austro-Hungarian Army Königlich und Kaiserlich Luftfahrtruppen (Royal and Imperial Air Service, or LFT). Of these 20 machines, 16 were built (53.01–53.16) before Oeffag's production focus also shifted to the D.III. Physically these D.II (Oef) machines resembled their German brethren, save for a few noteworthy exceptions. The first was the 185Ps Austro-Daimler Dm 185, an in-line, water-cooled, six-cylinder engine, fully enshrouded within metal cowl panels through which a coolant pipe protruded to the wing-mounted Daimler radiator. Later these cowls were removed to expose the cylinder heads to the slipstream and facilitate engine cooling. This engine was heavier than the 160Ps Mercedes D.III and required lengthening the wing chord by 10 cm to increase wing surface area. Armament consisted of a single synchronized 8mm Schwarzlose M07/12, internally mounted to starboard of the longitudinal axis; some machines also had one to port. A blast tube was connected to the barrel and extended through the engine compartment to prevent the accidental ignition of any accumulated gases within. This enclosed arrangement helped keep the gun better heated than if it had been mounted externally, but it also eliminated in-flight accessibility.

Mercedes DIII engine in Albatros D.II 1717/16. The triangular coolant expansion tank is above and to port of the rocker arm boxes, each located directly above a cylinder. The fuel tank air pressure pump protrudes at front, and the intake manifold is lagged with asbestos. Access hatches and louvres are forward of the Windhoff radiator, at right.

The M07/12 had its share of problems. A retarded blowback gun, the expanding propellant gases forced the cartridge case backwards out of the chamber. This required the bolt to be free to move backwards, and thus it was unlocked from the barrel and held in place via a recoil spring and inertia. An elbow joint attached to the bolt retarded its initial rearward movement and delayed opening the breech until the bullet had exited the barrel, but the powerful cartridges used still caused the breech to open too early. The barrel was shortened to allow the bullet to leave before the breech opened, but this reduced muzzle velocity and required a heavy bolt that limited rate of fire to 400 rounds per minute. Furthermore, the weapon was adversely affected by pressure changes that hampered the rate of fire and caused the weapon to stop firing when above 3,000m. Modifications to combat these problems led to the eventual development of the Schwarzlose M16.

Excluding prototypes, Albatros, OAW, LVG, and Oeffag built a total of 50 Albatros D.Is and 291 Albatros D.IIs. After their introduction to Western Front service in early September 1916, the D.I's front-line inventory peaked at 50 in October and then dwindled slowly; by the end of 1917 there were eight still in service. The D.IIs saw longer service times due to their greater production numbers, peaking at over 200 in December 1916 and sustaining this figure through February 1917, but after holding approximately three-quarters of their number through April the front-line inventory fell to six by the year's end. The 16 Albatros D.II (Oef)s saw Eastern Front service with various Fliegerkompagnien (Flying Companies, or Fliks) from May 1917.

160Ps Mercedes DIII on display at the Deutsches Museum Flugwerft Schleissheim, near Munich. (A) Coolant pipe connection; (B) rocker arm box; (C) intake valve and spring; (D) camshaft; (E) intake manifolds; (F) decompression lever; (G) water pump; (H) magneto; (I) oil pump and drain; (J) crankcase; (K) carburetor [absent]; (L) engine mount; (M) crankshaft; (N) water-jacketed cylinder; (O) priming petcock; (P) spark plug.

However, Flik 37/D recorded that the aeroplane's 'rapid climb has little effect because Russian aircraft practically never cross the lines; therefore the D.II mainly performs escort work.' Shortly after its appearance, the type was superseded by the D.III (Oef), with the D.II (Oef) relegated to a training machine, often for two-seater pilots transitioning to single-seaters. (See Osprey's *Austro-Hungarian Albatros Aces of World War 1*.)

TECHNICAL SPECIFICATIONS

The cornerstone of the Albatros D.I's and D.II's success was the 160Ps Daimler Mercedes F-1466 engine, commonly known as the Mercedes D.III. 'D' signified it was a product of Daimler Motoren Gesellschaft, Stuttgart-Untertürkheim, and 'III' was a Roman numeral that Idflieg assigned to signify performance range (0 was under 80Ps; I was 80–100Ps; II was 100–150Ps; III was 150–200Ps). It was a normally-aspirated, direct-drive, water-cooled, carbureted, in-line, overhead-cam, six-cylinder engine, cowled within detachable metal panels. Fuel tanks were located immediately aft; there was no firewall. Pilot engine management included a throttle mounted on the control column; a spark-retarding lever on the port cockpit wall, along with an engine magneto switch key and starting magneto crank; and an auxiliary throttle, located port-forward in the cockpit. Cooling was provided by fuselage-mounted radiators located just forward of the cockpit, with a triangular expansion tank fitted above the engine and slightly to port of the aeroplane's longitudinal axis. Early pre-production and all late-production D.IIs replaced these radiators and expansion tank with a single radiator centrally mounted within the upper wing, which was plumbed externally to carry coolant to and from the engine. This solid and reliable engine enabled the fully loaded D.I to attain a maximum speed of 109mph (175km/h) and climb to 13,123ft (4,000m) in 30 minutes.

The engine traced its roots to the 1913 Mercedes D.I engine, a 190kg (dry weight) in-line, water-cooled engine with six cylinders cast in pairs atop an aluminum crankcase, serviced by an overhead cam and two Bosch magnetos for dual ignition redundancy. Aeroplanes employing the Mercedes D.I included the LVG B I and Albatros B II. The following year brought the Mercedes D.II, which featured an increased bore from 120 to 125mm and augmented stroke from 140 to 150mm, increasing power output to 120Ps. The cylinders were still paired, although the cam tower was now enclosed and dry weight rose slightly to 210kg. Aeroplanes employing the Mercedes D.II included the LVG B I, Albatros B I and B II, and Fokker D.I.

In 1915 Daimler developed the Mercedes D.III. Pressed sheet steel water-jackets were welded to steel cylinders now bolted individually to a two-piece (upper and lower) sloped aluminium crankcase. These bolts passed through the upper crankcase half to attach to the lower, which not only secured the cylinders but aided securing the crankcase halves. Each cylinder featured single intake and exhaust ports and contained a four-ring piston machined from steel forgings; the compression ratio was 4.5:1. The valve gear was

contained within six aluminium-capped boxes through which rocker arms protruded to engage the intake and exhaust valves; these boxes were aligned above each cylinder and bolted to the camshaft. A two-barrel, twin-jet, updraft, float-type carburetor was positioned on the port side of the engine between the third and fourth cylinders and enclosed within a cast aluminium water jacket to prevent induction icing. Each carburetor throat fed a fuel–air mixture to three cylinders via branched steel tube intake manifolds that were often covered with asbestos cord lagging and bound with tape to prevent heat loss. Both throats were interconnected to the throttle but there was no altitude compensating mixture control for the pilot. Carburetor air intakes on the starboard side of the lower crankcase enabled internal oil cooling fins to warm the incoming air, further preventing induction icing, and fuel flow to the carburetor was initiated via a cylindrical camshaft-driven air pump that pressurized the main and emergency fuel tanks (80 and 23 litres, or 21.1 and 6.1 gallons respectively) located between the engine and the cockpit. Two Bosch Z.H.6 magnetos were affixed to the rear of the engine and driven by bevel gears off the vertical jackshaft that connected to the camshaft; the speed of the magnetos was 1.5 times that of the engine. Two Bosch spark plugs were fitted to each cylinder below the intake and exhaust valves and their associated wiring was routed through fibre tubes affixed horizontally to the cylinders. Cylinder firing order was 1, 5, 3, 6, 2, 4.

Top: Windhoff fuselage radiator. Affixed on each side of the nose, they could be fitted with extensions to increase their cooling capabilities. Conversely, in winter they could be partially covered to prevent overcooling. Bottom: Teeves and Braun wing radiator. This was centrally located and connected to the engine via externally plumbed pipes.

LEFT Methods used to plumb the D.II wing radiator varied. Top: OAW routed the coolant pipe down the port side of the engine, behind which it doglegged starboard to connect to the radiator. Bottom: Albatros routed the coolant pipe down the starboard side of the engine, which throughout the Albatros D series was more common.

RIGHT Garuda propeller on a D.II. Bottom: Axial propellers on D.Is, with early 'dagger' style logo (left) and later logo (right). Stamped data on blades or hubs imparted information pertinent to that propeller, such as expected engine type and power, diameter, pitch, manufacturer, and serial number. As with these examples, sometimes the stamps were filled with gold paint.

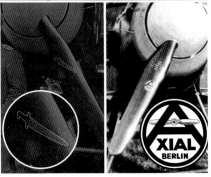

Mercedes D.III (D-1466) Engine Specifications	
Bore	140mm
Stroke	160mm
Compression Ratio	4.5:1
Average bhp and speed	162.5 at 1400rpm
Total dry engine weight*	618lb
Weight per bhp	3.8lb
Fuel consumption per hour	11.75gal
*Excludes propeller hub and exhaust manifold	

A Maxim IMG 08/15 machine gun with belted 7.62mm ammunition. All Albatros D models were equipped with two of these weapons synchronized to fire through the propeller arc. Maximum firing rate was 450 rounds per minute, although this changed with the variable speed of the propeller blades.

Engine cooling for the Albatros D.I and early D.IIs was provided by two side-mounted (one port, one starboard) Windhoff radiators, boxy structures mounted to the fuselage approximately on the thrust line and adjacent the aft engine cowlings. A triangular expansion tank (also known as a header tank) was fitted above the engine and slightly to port of the longitudinal axis and provided space for coolant expansion when hot. At some point within the third D.II production batch (D.1700–1799) the Windhoff 'ear' radiators were replaced with a Teeves and Braun wing-mounted radiator that was centrally

located between the D.II's central N-struts. There was no specific moment when this occurred, but rather a gradual blend during construction, with some machines outfitted with Windhoff radiators and some with a Teeves and Braun. Based on photographs, examples of this blend include:

D.1712/16	Windhoff
D.1717/16	Windhoff
D.1724/16	Windhoff
D.1727/16	Teeves and Braun
D.1729/16	Teeves and Braun
D.1742/16	Teeves and Braun
D.1743/16	Teeves and Braun
D.1746/16	Teeves and Braun
D.1753/16	Windhoff
D.1756/16	Teeves and Braun
D.1765/16	Windhoff
D.1768/16	Teeves and Braun
D.1769/16	Teeves and Braun
D.1774/16	Windhoff
D.1774/16	Windhoff
D.1782/16	Teeves and Braun
D.1784/16	Teeves and Braun
D.1789/16	Windhoff
D.1799/16	Teeves and Braun

This blend is also seen with machines licence-built by OAW and LVG, although on many OAW machines outfitted with a Teeves and Braun radiator the associated external coolant pipe was connected to the port side of the first cylinder's water jacket and plumbed down the port side of the engine, aft of which it doglegged to starboard and connected to the starboard side of the wing radiator. This was contrary to the practice of Albatros- and LVG-built machines, which plumbed their external coolant pipes entirely to starboard.

For coolant, Daimler recommended that soft water (water free of minerals, particularly lime, which can foul plumbing) be used, and specified the allowance of pure rainwater, boiled water, or distilled water; all had to be filtered prior to use. During cold weather, hot water was to be used, with glycerine or denatured alcohol added; a 60–70 per cent blend of glycerine lowered the freezing point of water to -36°F (-37.8°C). Coolant circulation was via a water pump located above the magnetos and driven off the vertical jackshaft, with pump lubrication conducted by hand via a pilot-controlled, screw-down grease lubricator.

All engine parts were lubricated with oil supplied by an oil pump, which was driven by the lower vertical jackshaft at the bottom rear of the engine. The main oil circuit fed the crankshaft and camshaft bearings, while a supplementary circuit drew fresh oil from the oil tank and continually fed it into the system. An auxiliary suction pump drew oil away from the system and returned it to the oil tank.

Engine access for maintenance and servicing was somewhat limited by the close engine cowling, but these panels could be removed easily and had a round hatch to port that allowed access to the carburetor, as did a hatch on the port fuselage. The starboard engine cowl had no access hatch but there was one below on the fuselage, and several hatches under the nose granted access to the carburetor air intakes, oil drain, oil line, and oil pump on the bottom of

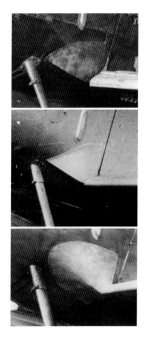

These modern D.II reproduction fuselages under construction afford an excellent view of how wing root fairings blended the slab-sided wing junctions with the ovoid fuselage nose sections. (Photograph courtesy of Koloman Mayrhofer)

Different Albatros manufacturers employed wing root fairings of subtle design variations. From top to bottom: Johannisthal, OAW, Oeffag. LVG fairings were similar to or the same as those of Johannisthal, which along with OAW fairings were made from two pieces of either wood or metal. Oeffag fairings were shaped from a single piece of engine-turned aluminium.

the engine. Also, six staggered metal louvres – three each on the nose, port and starboard – promoted airflow circulation through the engine compartment to remove excess heat and prevent potentially volatile gases from accumulating.

After examining a 160Ps Mercedes D.III engine from a captured Albatros D.I, the 13 January 1916 issue of the British aero weekly *Flight* stated the following:

If we are not altogether enamoured of the design ... the workmanship and finish embodied in the Mercedes are, on the other hand, such as to excite admiration, for they are certainly of the very finest. Moreover ... it is very evident that reliability almost to the exclusion of all else has been the object sought after. This is revealed by the 'heftiness' of every internal working part; even in the reciprocating members little or no effort seems to have been made to cut down weight to an extent likely to influence reliability. On the contrary, it is clear the designers have, as we suggested above, been content to limit revolutions, and by doing so take the advantage permitted to increase the factor of safety, the result being that the Mercedes – as it undoubtedly is – is an engine comparable with an ordinary car engine in the matter of infrequent need for attention and overhaul, long life, and unfailing service except for accident.

It must not be thought from this, however, that the question of weight reduction has not received any consideration whatever. On the contrary, it has evidently been carefully studied, although this is a fact that is not by any means obvious from the

C

1. ALBATROS D.I
The Albatros D.I's inverted-V struts were a design feature culled from their successful B- and C-type two-seaters, and were only associated with the first of their D-types. Although structurally sound, the struts placed the upper wings in a position that created a blind spot to the front and above. The converging struts also hindered vision needed for stalking prey and aiming machine guns – vision already marred by the protruding radiator expansion tank.

2. ALBATROS D.II WITH WINDHOFF RADIATORS
The Albatros D.II improved vision by replacing the converging inverted-V struts with diverging N-struts. This lowered the wings and lessened the blind spot above while opening the forward vision, with less need for ducking around struts. The Windhoff radiators and associated expansion tank remained, but overall cockpit vision had been improved.

3. ALBATROS D.II WITH TEEVES AND BRAUN RADIATOR
Albatros continually refined their D-type design. Soon the Windhoff radiators were replaced by a single Teeves and Braun airfoil radiator, centrally located in the upper wing, with a smaller expansion tank protruding above. Note that each cylinder exhaust port connected to an independent manifold that led to a single manifold that channelled exhaust gases away from the pilot. Albatros Ds were not fitted with mufflers.

4. ALBATROS D.II WITH BECKER CANNON
In November 1916 Albatros conducted firing trials with a 20mm Becker cannon installed in an Albatros D.II, mounted to the bracket that normally supported the Maxim machine guns (removed from this machine, likely to compensate for the Becker's 73lb [33kg] weight). Researcher Peter Grosz wrote that this configuration may have undergone front-line evaluation in December, but a cannon-equipped D.II never entered production.

5. ALBATROS D.II (OEF)
The 16 Austrian-built D.IIs largely resembled those built in Germany. Noticeable differences included a fully cowled engine (which was removed in warmer weather to combat overheating), an additional fuselage hatch to facilitate fuelling, a more rounded wing root fairing, and prodigious use of engine-turned or jewelled metal.

Although grainy, this is a rare view of an Albatros D.I's framework. Engine, cowl panels, and armament have been removed, but the cylindrical oil tank remains in the nose. The fuel tank is visible behind the attachment plate for the Windhoff radiator. Wing rib lightening holes are evident, as is the absence of wire bracing throughout the fuselage.

exterior. It is in respect to the parts that may be considered as the framework rather than the working parts of the engine that the endeavours in this direction have been directed, especially the crankcase and the cylinders, though nowhere has the achievement of the object been allowed to interfere with the rigidity of the engine as a whole, and therefore with its smooth running potentialities.

The Mercedes D.III turned a fixed-pitch, two-blade, wooden propeller consisting of several 6–20mm thick boards that had been glued together so that the grain of each board ran diagonally to the next, which prevented twisting. Preferred woods included walnut, ash, mahogany, and teak, but eventual import shortages necessitated also using maple, elm, and pine. The latter was avoided as far as possible because as a softwood it was too sensitive to rain, hail, sand, and dust erosion; if used, pine required special protection. During construction the various wood laminations were heated to 100°F (38°C) to enhance the permeability of the freshly made animal glue, which after application was allowed to penetrate the wood before the laminations were clamped together for 24 hours. Afterwards the centre bore hole and bolt holes were drilled to better than a half-millimetre accuracy, adherence to which was especially important for use with machine gun synchronization systems. The propeller blades were shaped by hand using guide templates to ensure accuracy, sanded, and then received multiple coats of shellac and varnish. Shellac is not waterproof and was probably used to seal the wood grain as an undercoat for the varnish, which protected the propeller from delamination due to moisture.

Axial propellers were commonly seen on Albatros D.Is and D.IIs, as were those of Garuda and Reschke, but regardless of manufacturer the propeller hubs were enclosed within a large aerodynamic spinner (of a slightly smaller diameter than the fuselage to allow entry of cooling air into the engine compartment) that could be removed for preventative or reparative maintenance access. Idflieg's 1916 *Propellermerkbuch* (Propeller Notebook) stipulated that all propellers were to be kept clean, with the wood and metal parts greased strongly for moisture protection, especially in damp weather and after flights in fog or rain. Problems lurked even in good weather:

> In continuously dry weather the wood of the propeller shrinks; in damp weather it expands. After each weather change therefore the propeller should be examined to see if it sits correctly on the engine hub. If necessary, the nuts on the mounting bolts are to be tightened. If the weather is damp, then the bolts are to be loosened, then retightened correctly, otherwise the propeller can crack by the expansion of the wood at the hub or damage the mounting bolts.

Additionally, flight damage from raindrops or hail and erosion from sand and small pebbles picked up during ground operations degraded propeller performance and required the damaged blade be 'sanded off and repainted on the aircraft, an easy task'. This led to the dark appearance of some propellers, although photographs also reveal that between sorties the propeller blades were often ensconced within protective sheaths. More significant damage to the leading and trailing edges of propellers could be repaired via a wooden plug that was glued into a trapezoidal excision of the damaged portion of the blade, with the wider portion of the wedge-shaped plug closer to the blade centre to prevent the plug from flying out due to rotational forces. The notebook also stated that

> the 160Ps Mercedes engines have a critical period at 1320 to 1340rpm when the engine vibrates strongly. With these engines one selects carefully propellers that can make 1400 to 1460rpm in flight. If a suitable propeller is not to hand, then one can cut off without hesitation up to 3cm off each blade. Reducing the diameter by around 1cm increases the speed by 6 to 10rpm. With smooth running engines this measure is not necessary.

The Albatros D.I and D.II's armament consisted of two fixed and forward-firing Maxim lMG 08/15 7.92mm air-cooled machine guns, each synchronized to fire 500 rounds through the propeller arc. Colloquially known as a 'Spandau' due to its manufacture at Königlich Gewehr und Munitions Fabrik (Royal Gun and Munitions Factory) of Spandau, Berlin, the weapon's lineage traces back to its 1884 invention by Hiram Maxim, an American from Sangerville, Maine, who worked in London and eventually became a naturalized British subject. His machine gun utilized a belt-fed and recoil-operated design in which the barrel and bolt recoiled together a few millimetres before the barrel stopped and the bolt continued rearward to extract and eject the fired cartridge and cock the firing pin. A return spring pushed the bolt back toward the breech, chambering the next cartridge and locking in place to be fired again.

The Maxim and its variants saw greatest use by the German army, which adopted the weapon as the MG 08, in its standard 7.92 x 57mm (measurements of the cartridge case) military rifle calibre. With the development of the technique of fixing machine guns to aeroplanes and synchronizing them to fire forward through a spinning propeller arc in 1915, the Maxim's precise firing made it an ideal weapon for this purpose. However, since it was originally water-cooled, the weight associated with the water-jacketed barrel was detrimental to aeroplane performance and required a conversion to air-

A depiction of how an angled scarf joint increased the surface area to be glued, resulting in a stronger marriage than if the pieces had been glued via an end-on butt joint. Albatros seams were reinforced internally with fabric and did not necessarily align with formers when glued and nailed to the airframe.

cooling. The seemingly obvious solution was to remove the water jacket, but since it supported the barrel as it moved back and forth during firing, the jacket was instead drained of water and its front and sides perforated to allow the circulation of cooling air. Subsequent designs included removing unnecessary parts and replacing the water jacket with a perforated jacket of reduced diameter. This weapon became known as the lMG 08/15.

Synchronized to fire 500 rounds between the rotating propeller blades at a maximum rate of 450 rounds per minute, one must remember that this rate was dependent upon engine speed and varied with different propeller rpms, as the synchronization gear compensated for the variable frequency with which the blades passed before the gun muzzles. The standard synchronization gear used by German aeroplane manufacturers was the Fokker Zentralsteuerung (central control) system. This was a natural progression from the initial Stangensteuerung (pushrod control) system, which was actually an 'interrupter gear' comprised of pushrods and mechanical linkages driven by a rotating cam connected to the engine crankshaft or camshaft that prevented (interrupted) the weapon from firing whenever the blades passed before the muzzle. The Zentralsteuerung system replaced the rigid pushrods, which were susceptible to contraction due to frigid temperatures at altitude, with a flexible drive shaft that rotated a cam and engaged a spring-loaded pin that pushed the trigger, permitting gunfire synchronized with the blades when they were clear of the

Albatros D.I cockpit. Engine and starting magnetos are at left, twin-grip control column with central triggers is at right. Efforts to minimize drag are exemplified by the faired inverted-V struts, atop which the wings are in the forward stagger position. Had these V-struts been retained with the Albatros D.II's lowered wings, their convergence would have hampered the forward vision needed for stalking and attacking.

gun muzzles, as opposed to an interrupter system preventing gunfire when the blades were not clear. The end result was the same, although synchronization was more reliable and efficient than interruption.

Despite the Fokker Zentralsteuerung system being furnished to all German aeroplane manufacturers, Albatros chose instead to devise and utilize an in-house two-gun synchronization mechanism that comprised a cam and oscillating rods, designed by Werkmeister Hedtke and eventually modified by Werkmeister Semmler. This decision raised Idflieg concerns that multiple synchronization systems would complicate armourer training, but Albatros remained committed to the Hedtke system, having apparently tested Fokker's Zentralsteuerung system in October 1916 and deeming said testing to be unsuccessful. Still, Idflieg considered the Zentralsteuerung system to be superior.

Triggers were centrally located on the control column and situated so the guns could be fired separately or simultaneously. Gun breeches were pilot-accessible for cocking and clearing jams. Hemp-belted cartridges were stored in magazines forward of the cockpit and fed to the guns via curved metal chutes. After passing through the guns, the empty belts descended separate chutes (which on the port side were covered by an aerodynamic fairing called a *Beule* or bump on Johannisthal- and LVG-built machines, although this was absent on OAW builds) to collect in bins adjacent the magazines; cartridge cases were ejected overboard. As with the engines, the guns were partially cowled within detachable metal panels.

The Albatros D.I and D.II fuselages were identical and featured a circular nose and slab-sided cross-section that flowed smoothly into an ovoid top and underside, with the ovoid transitions becoming more knife-edged as they neared the empennage. The intersection of the curved belly and slab-sided fuselage at the lower-wing leading and trailing edge connection points created drag-producing protuberances that required the installation of either wood or metal aerodynamic fairings. The fuselage was of semi-monocoque construction, whereby the external skin acted in concert with the frame to share the stress of external loads, resulting in great strength without the need for internal wire bracing. The wooden frame employed six longerons, three each port and starboard. The centre longerons were ¾ inch x ¾ inch L-sections forward of the cockpit and ¾ inch x 5/16 inch spruce rectangular sections from there aft. The upper and lower longerons were largely 1 3/16 inch x 1 9/16 inch ash L-sections up to the cockpit, with spruce employed from there aft, along which

ABOVE LEFT Albatros D.II cockpit. Increased forward vision gained by the outwardly-splayed N struts is evident. Fuel control valves are located at right, beneath the Maxim support bar, onto which a non-standard clock has been affixed. The tachometer is obscured well forward, while the control column and its triggers and throttle are well lighted. Note the rear view mirror, Maxim Beule, and external flare stowage at left. The curved dark object at right is the exhaust manifold.

ABOVE RIGHT Albatros D.II (Oef) cockpit. The manual fuel tank air pump is at centre bottom. Above that are the magneto switch key, starter magneto, liquid inclinometer, and tachometer. The control column is pushed forward and provides a view of its locking device. Note the small windscreen on the aerodynamically clean fuselage, attained by mounting weapons internally (although this particular machine is unarmed).

ground wires were channelled rearwards from the engine mounts to the cabane strut mounts (which channelled the ground to a wire in the upper wing), tail-post tube and horizontal stabilizer. Connected to the longerons were 3/8-inch-thick simple transverse formers spaced approximately every two feet, with four transverse supports employed as engine bearers forward of the cockpit. The entire frame was treated with shellac.

Covering this frame was a sectioned 2–3mm three-ply birch plywood skin that had been pressed into compound shapes in moulds and then glued together via bevelled scarf-joints that increased the surface area to be glued, providing a stronger connection than if the two pieces had been simply glued end-to-end. These scarf-jointed seams were internally reinforced with glued strips of heavy-weave cotton fabric and the resultant large shells were then glued and nailed to the formers and stringers, with the corners secured by screws. Glue was the primary bond for joining the structure; the steel nails and screws were used to hold the structure in place as the glue cured, but they also provided additional strength. When attached to the frame the scarf-joint seams did not necessarily align with the locations of the formers and typically were offset. Both sides of the skin received multiple coats of shellac and varnish, producing the oft-noted 'warm straw-yellow' appearance and gleaming high-gloss sheen.

The Albatros D.I and D.II employed a high-sided, ovoid-shaped open cockpit, with edges strengthened by a double thickness of wood and covered with a padded leather coaming, with a small windscreen forward that shielded the pilot from the slipstream.

Entry was assisted by a single rounded sprung-door footstep located on the lower port longeron, although normally pilots gained the cockpit via a ladder and ground crew assistance, and it is reasonable to speculate that the footstep was meant more as a means of exit assistance rather than entry. The cockpit interior was much more spacious and protective of the elements than those of French and British machines, and the lack of a firewall enabled the Albatros pilots to enjoy the warming benefits of radiant engine heat that frigid RFC (Royal Flying Corps) pusher crews could only dream about.

The pilot sat in an upholstered bucket seat, adjustable fore and aft, with security provided by a four-point seatbelt and shoulder harness restraint, although instead of securing the pilot directly across his legs the wide seatbelt fastened across the top of the bucket seat. This helped prevent him from falling from the machine, but the shoulder harness provided the bulk of pilot security. Control of pitch and roll was conducted via a metal control column with two wooden hand grips that straddled the left and right machine gun triggers, allowing them to be engaged via the thumbs. Cables leading to the guns were plumbed externally from the column's hollow core, as was the cable leading to the primary engine throttle clamped to the left hand grip. There was no trim to relieve the pilot of any control pressures, but a locking device on the control column could be engaged to permit a brief measure of hands-off flying, by preventing fore and aft control movement (elevator control) while still allowing lateral movement (aileron control). A conventional rudder bar with metal toe straps enabled control of yaw about the vertical axis, although there were neither toe brakes, rudder trim, nor tailskid steering.

Close-up of a captured D.I's cabane struts. The missing upper wing reveals the holes through which bolts passed to lock upper wing eyebolts seated in slots at the top of the struts, allowing adjustment of stagger. Note how the exhaust manifold straddles the forward cabane strut. Rather than a triangular expansion tank, this D.I featured a rare conical version ahead of the first cylinder, indicating it was one of the pre-production machines, one of perhaps only two so equipped.

Flight and navigation instrumentation in the Albatros cockpit was sparse, especially when compared with RFC machines; there was no 'instrument panel' as is commonplace today. Instead, a centrally located tachometer was attached to the metal support of the Maxim breeches, with a fuel pressure gauge behind and to the right of that frame, and a fuel quantity gauge was located on the starboard cockpit wall. An altimeter and airspeed indicator could be present (the latter was an anemometer type and commonly but not exclusively located on an interplane strut), but these were retrofitted installations and not factory standard. The sole navigational instrument was a floor-mounted magnetic compass. This was a less than ideal location for navigating via precise headings, but Albatros pilots did not conduct long-range A-to-B navigation often. Instead, they employed pilotage (using fixed visual ground references like roads, lakes, woods, roads, railroads, and villages to guide oneself to a destination) for local short-range navigation over known territories and locales, as they were hunting enemy aeroplanes in a familiar geographical area, not finding their way crosscountry to distant locales beyond the horizon. Thus the compass mostly provided a measure of general orientation, such as could be useful after a combat mêlée during which navigation had been ignored in favour of fighting and survival; a pilot could reference the compass and turn in the general direction for home until such time as he identified local landmarks familiar to him.

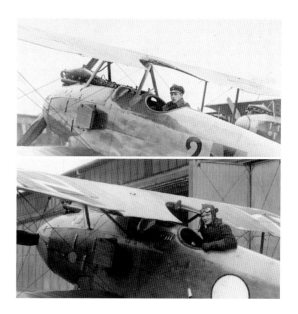

What the Albatros lacked in flight instrumentation it made up for with engine and fuel controls, three of which were mounted on the port cockpit wall. The first was the engine magneto switch key, which was attached to a chain and removable for safety; in some photographs it can be seen dangling outside the cockpits of parked machines. This switch could be placed in four positions. At position 0 the engine-driven magnetos and the starting magneto were off; at position M1 (for starting) the left magneto and starting magneto were on; at position M2 the left magneto was off, while the right magneto and starting magneto were on; and in position 2 both engine-driven magnetos and the starting magneto were on. Next to the magneto switch key was the spark-retarding lever. Often mistaken for the throttle today, this lever allowed the pilot to delay the timing of when the spark plugs fired, compensating for slower piston travel at idling or low engine speeds as compared to piston speeds at cruise or full power settings.

Forward and below this lever was the starting magneto crank. Although the Albatros D.I and D.II required ground assistance for engine starts, they did not employ personnel to 'swing' the propeller as did aeroplanes with rotary engines. Instead, ground crew filled the cylinder petcocks with a mixture of oil and benzene, slowly pulled the propeller through several

This comparison demonstrates the difference between the D.I's inverted-V cabane struts and the D.II's splayed-N struts. The D.II's reduced wing gap is clearly evident. Note that the D.II's aft cabane attachment point is further forward than the D.I's.

Development of the Albatros D empennage. The D.I prototype at left utilized externally routed rudder control cables, as did the elevator, which was unbalanced. The D.I and D.II production machines (the latter at right) used internally routed aileron cables that required service access hatches near the rudderpost. The elevator was balanced, and the tailskid ventral fin received an external brace along its underside.

Tailskid on an Albatros D.II (Oeffag). Rounded where bungeed for shock absorption, it became slab-sided at the aft connection point where the steel-shoe began. This shoe enabled tailskids to 'plough' into aerodrome turf and soil, helping slow the machine and prevent ground loops.

Starboard axle–landing gear strut connection on a D.II. The axle fitted inside the 'V' strut and was secured by wrapped bungees that bore the weight of the aeroplane. The loop above the bungees was a steel restraining cable that supported the machine in case of bungee failure, preventing the strut apex from digging into the ground and overturning the aeroplane.

complete revolutions to draw the priming fuel into the cylinders, and then the pilot positioned the magneto switch key to M1 and rapidly hand-cranked the starting magneto. This created a continuous spark discharge in the cylinder at or past top dead-centre, igniting the fuel–air mixture and driving the piston downward. This action caused the engine-driven magnetos to fire the spark plugs in the other cylinders, starting the engine and engaging the engine-driven air pump that continuously pressurized the fuel tank to send fuel to the carburetor, thereby completing the self-sustaining cycle.

The front of the Albatros cockpit was comprised mostly of the cartridge-belt container and ammunition storage bins, but protruding from the upper left side was an auxiliary throttle handle, which was a horizontal metal rod with a looped end. In the event of primary throttle control abnormality (e.g. if the control cable were severed by enemy bullets), the pilot could push the auxiliary throttle fully forward until a detent at the end of the rod locked the auxiliary throttle to the carburetor, thereby restoring throttle control.

Fuel control valves were located on the right side of the cockpit, where a wooden panel supported a fuel pressure gauge valve control, air pump selector valve, fuel tank air pressure valve, and a fuel tank flow selector valve. For normal engine start and flight procedures, these valve handles all pointed downward and required little pilot attention. However, the pilot was afforded a measure of flexibility between the main and emergency fuel tanks if the need arose. Setting the fuel tank air pressure valve to *Emergency Tank* and the fuel tank flow selector valve to *Emergency Fuel* enabled fuel to flow from the emergency tank to the carburetor. Moving the fuel tank flow selector valve to *Emergency Fuel Filling* allowed fuel to flow to the carburetor but also to the main tank, where total fuel quantity could be read from the fuel gauge that measured the main tank only (assuming pilots trusted this gauge was accurate). Below the fuel valve panel, a hand-operated air pump allowed the pilot to pressurize the fuel tanks for starting (prior to pressurization from the engine-driven air pump) or when the engine-driven air pump was inoperative.

Lastly, a water pump greaser was installed on the far starboard side that the pilot twisted a half-turn every ten minutes to ensure proper water pump lubrication.

Lift for the Albatros D.I and D.II was provided by two equal and constant chord, wooden-framed, wire-braced, subtly tip-tapered, single-bay wings of slightly unequal span. These were covered with a skin of doped fabric and affixed to the aeroplane with positive stagger but without dihedral or sweepback, although the trailing edges of the ailerons were raked slightly aft. The frame consisted of two fabric-bound, rectangular wooden spars situated approximately 2 feet 8 inches apart, held in alignment via steel compression bars (to which a ground wire was

attached) and turnbuckle-adjusted crosswires. The basswood ribs were capped with ash, employed prodigious lightening holes, and were situated 16¼ inches apart on the upper wing and 13¾ inches apart on the lower wings, between which intermediate ribs extended back to the aft main spar. The ribs were joined by a span-wise rounded cap strip to form the leading edge, and their ends were connected via an approximately 1mm wire that formed the trailing edge of the wing. The upper and lower wings were connected via pairs of wire-braced interplane struts located outboard port and starboard, one pair on each side. The struts were streamlined steel tube and were connected to the upper and lower spars. These spars, as with all wooden components of the wings, were varnished for moisture protection.

The frame was covered in swatches of linen fabric sewn to 5mm-wide strips of reinforcement tape that had been tied to the upper and lower cap strips of each rib. Stitching was accomplished via overhand loops secured by half hitches, spaced approximately 30mm apart along the ribs; once complete, the stitching was covered by strips of 25mm-wide finishing tape; no finishing tape was used on Oeffag machines. The wings then received applications of dope that weatherproofed the fabric and rendered it taut, causing it to pull against the trailing edge wire and create the classic scalloped appearance associated with many World War I machines. For pilot control of roll, fabric-covered steel frame ailerons were attached to an auxiliary spar located behind the aft main spar, on the outer port and starboard portions of the upper wing only. Control cables descended vertically behind the aft interplane struts and into the lower wings, through which they were routed to the control column.

The method by which the upper wings were attached to the fuselage via the cabane struts differed between the D.I and D.II. On the D.I they were attached via inverted V-struts just forward of the cockpit, similar to the method employed on Albatros C-types. The upper wing stagger could be adjusted from 0 to 12cm by moving the wing along the top of the inverted V-strut, in which a slot on each end received an eyebolt passing through the forward main spar of the wing. Each slot was co-located with five holes, one of which received a bolt that locked the upper wing eyebolt in the location of desired stagger, which photographs reveal was often fully forward.

To improve forward visibility, the inverted V-struts of the D.I were replaced by outwardly-splayed N-struts on the D.II; these struts were utilized thereafter

Johannisthal-built Albatros D.II 1724/16, 25th machine of the third production batch. Salient details include overpainted upper wing crossfields; lagged intake manifolds that are 'blast wrapped' to protect from machine gun muzzle-flash; anemometer on the port interplane strut; soft-blended camouflage demarcations on lower wings; mirror in upper wing cutout; flares near cockpit; and a field-modified flare tube through the port cockpit wall. The pilot is future Orden Pour le Mérite-decorated, 30-victory ace Ltn Karl Emil Schaefer.

OAW-built Albatros D.II (OAW) 910/16, 21st machine of the second production batch. Salient details include Garuda propeller; OAW's rough camouflage demarcations; starboard-plumbed coolant pipe; dark longeron seam; manufacture placards near cockpit; no serial number on vertical stabilizer. This Jasta 5 machine was shot down and captured on 4 March 1917, with Ltn Max Böhme becoming a PoW.

on all subsequent Albatros models. Furthermore, to improve upward visibility from the cockpit, the D.II's upper wing was lowered 250mm (9.8in), reducing wing gap from 1.6m (5ft 3in) on the D.I to 1.35m (4ft 5in) on the D.II. As mentioned previously, this alteration was not the result of combat experience, but was first seen on the pre-production D.II, which had been built before D.I production had even begun.

The wood-framed empennage featured a ply-covered vertical stabilizer and two fabric-covered horizontal stabilizers, all of which employed curved leading edges and low aspect ratios. The steel tube-framed, counterbalanced rudder and one-piece elevator were covered with doped fabric and operated via cables routed through the fuselage and into the cockpit. The rudder post bellcrank and connecting cables were housed completely within the fuselage, and for servicing required the installation of port and starboard access hatches near the trailing edge of the vertical stabilizer, above the horizontal stabilizers. The empennage undersurface featured a wood-framed and three-ply-skinned triangular ventral fin that not only aided lateral stability about the vertical axis but also housed a one-piece, steel-shoed, ash tailskid in the 'bee-stinger' position that was bungeed for a measure of shock absorption. Due to the need for strength in this area, the ventral fin received a duel covering of three-ply birch, which created a total skin thickness of 4mm.

Albatros D.II (Oef) 53.15, the penultimate machine of the 16 D.IIs built by Oeffag. Salient details include the Daimler 185 engine (exposed here, it could also be completely enclosed within the cowling); high-plumbed coolant pipe; hatches for fuel tank and valve access; clear-doped-lined wings and tail, void of camouflage; fat, borderless cross and prominent serial number on fuselage; and tail cross confined to the rudder.

Similarly, the main landing gear employed bungeed shock absorption that also served to connect the struts to the wheel axle, upon which revolved two 760 x 100mm covered disc wheels with rectangular valve access hatches; a steel restraining cable was used to limit axle travel and prevented gear collapse in the event of bungee failure.

The struts were streamlined steel tubes arranged in a conventional 'V' configuration that inserted into tubular port and starboard sockets bolted and strapped to the curved underside of the fuselage nose, as well as bolted to the belly between the wings. The rear struts were cable-braced. A transverse tubular tie rod was located behind the axle, and although both the axle and tie rod were enclosed within a wood aerodynamic fairing on the future Albatros models, the D.I and D.II did not employ such an enclosure.

Performance specifications for the various D.I and D.II builds were fairly consistent between the types. Official D.II specs list it as 46lb (21kg) lighter than the D.I – ostensibly this refers to the late-production D.IIs that had one instead of two radiators, as well as shortened interplane struts – and thus the D.II had a slightly better rate of climb, although overall both models were sleek and rugged war machines. More powerful than their single-seat adversaries, they had better firepower, more reliable engines, and cockpits that provided much more pilot protection from the elements. With these machines the Germans took tactical control of the Western Front skies in autumn 1916 and passed that baton to the D.I and D.II successor, the Albatros D.III, which, although hamstrung initially with significant structural teething troubles, continued to hold sway over the RFC through the middle of 1917.

Factory Finishes and Idiosyncracies

Although produced by three different manufacturing companies in Germany (Albatros Flugzeugwerke, Johannisthal; Ostdeutsche Albatros Werke [OAW], Schneidmühl; Luftverkehrsgesellschaft [LVG], Johannisthal) that used camouflage variations, most production Albatros D.Is and D.IIs employed a high-gloss shellacked and varnished birch fuselage that has been described as appearing 'warm straw-yellow'. The spinner, engine cowling panels, fittings, access hatches, vents, and cabane, interplane, and undercarriage struts were either light grey, pale greenish-grey, or greenish-beige. The wheel covers and undersurfaces of the wings, ailerons, horizontal stabilizers and elevator were light blue, but the uppersurfaces and national markings varied between the individual manufacturers.

Albatros Flugzeugwerke (D.I 422–471/16; D.II 472–521/16; D.II 1700–1799/16)

Johannisthal-built production D.I and D.II wing uppersurfaces employed a two-tone camouflage of Venetian red and olive green or three-tone camouflage of Venetian red, olive green, and pale green; the pattern of camouflage colours and their port or starboard directional slant varied between machines. Wing undersurfaces were pale blue. The fabric-covered rudder could be either clear doped linen or often one of the various camouflage colours. Again, this varied between machines.

National markings consisted of a black Eisernkreuz (Iron Cross) on a square white crossfield at eight points: one at each upper wing uppersurface wingtip and each lower wing undersurface wingtip (although some lower wing crosses were applied directly to the pale blue undersurfaces without a white crossfield or border); one on each side of the fuselage, well aft near the horizontal stabilizer; and one each side of the tail, overlapping the hinge line of the vertical stabilizer and the rudder. The upper wing crossfields were centred slightly inboard

Planform camouflage views of the various D.II manufacturers. From the top: Albatros, with sloping, feather-blended, irregular bands of olive green, pale green, and venetian red; OAW, with large, roughly-blended patches of 'burnt sienna and light and dark green'; LVG, with mirrored, blended bands of burnt sienna, dark green, and light Brunswick green; Oeffag, clear doped linen *sans* camouflage.

LVG-built Albatros D.II. These machines resembled those built by Albatros. Differences include the absence of a serial number on the tail and a subtly applied weights table near the lower wing junction. Note the wing cut-out mirror, flares near the cockpit, and LVG's strong, banded camouflage pattern on the lower wing. (Photo courtesy of DEHLA Collection)

the interplane struts and were not quite full chord, stretching instead from the leading edge to several inches shy of the trailing edge. A black serial number such as 'D.481/16' was hand-painted on either side of the vertical stabilizer ('D' represented the aircraft designation, single-engined single-seat biplane with armament, and '481' denoted it was the tenth machine of the first production batch, D.472–521/16; and '/16' was the last two digits of the year the machine was ordered and thus, although similar, no two numbers were exactly alike). Manufacturer and Idflieg placards were located on either side of the nose and on the leading edge of the lower wings, just outboard of the interplane struts. Finally, an Albatros company logo (a helmeted bird with wings spread in flight) adorned each side of the rudder and was applied so that both port and starboard birds faced (i.e. 'flew toward') the spinner.

Additionally, some Albatrosses had their fuselages camouflaged in bands of olive green and rust brown, and the fuselage bottom painted pale blue with a subtly feathered demarcation between the upper and lower surfaces. Furthermore, other Albatros fuselages may have been stained reddish-brown, based on an Idflieg document stating 'experiments by the Albatros firm have

D

1. ALBATROS D.I, SERIAL NO. U/K, FLOWN BY PRINCE FRIEDRICH KARL OF PRUSSIA, JASTA BOELCKE, ESWARS, MARCH 1917

One of the pre-production Albatrosses received by Jasta 2, this Albatros D.I was seconded to Prince Friedrich Karl of Flieger-Abteilung (A) 258, in anticipation of his pending transfer into Jasta Boelcke. One of only two or three D.Is with an expansion tank ahead of the cylinders, this machine was painted green (exact shade unknown) and flown by Ltn Diether Collin until given to the prince, who eventually emblazoned the fuselage and spinner with his previous regiment's 'Death Head' insignia. Forced to land with a shot-up engine on 21 March 1917 – the prince was mortally wounded while running toward German lines – it is depicted here as photographed post-capture, without wings and horizontal stabilizers, although their unpainted wood outlines remain.

2. ALBATROS D.II (LVG), SERIAL NO. U/K, FLOWN BY LTN ROBERT DYCKE, JASTA 16B, ENSISHEIM, MARCH 1917

One of several LVG-built Albatros D.IIs received by Jasta 16b ('b' denotes the Staffel's Bavarian association), this machine was flown by Ltn Robert Dycke, who became Staffelführer later that August. Jasta 16b Albatros D.II did not employ squadron recognition markings, but featured personal decoration on the fuselage, which on Dycke's machine was the Kleines Wappen des Freistaates Bayern (lesser coat of arms of the freestate of Bavaria) within a black-bordered white diamond. Otherwise, the aeroplane appeared LVG factory standard, replete with a weights table on the fuselage and absence of serial number on the tail.

3. ALBATROS D.II (OAW), 910/16, FLOWN BY LTN MAX BÖHME, JASTA 5, BOISTRANCOURT, MARCH 1917

This OAW-built D.II featured factory-camouflaged fuselage and wings, light blue undersurfaces, and had the numeral '8' painted on the top, bottom, and both sides of the fuselage between the Eisernkreuz and cockpit. On 4 March 1917, Ltn Max Böhme was flying 910/16 when brought down behind Allied lines. His D.II was captured intact and assigned the British capture number G 14. Eventually, it was transferred to the French and renumbered AL 910. Depicted here in French ownership, the now unarmed D.II was painted in silver *enduit metallisé* (like the Nieuport 17) and sported French wing roundels and a tricoloured tail. Also, the original Garuda propeller was replaced by a Levasseur.

4. ALBATROS D.II (OEF), 53.06, FLICKS 37D AND 50D, MID–LATE 1917

The sixth of 16 Albatros D.IIs built by the Hungarians, 53.06 appeared in Oeffag's typically Spartan factory finish. Depicted here when testing a German Teeves and Braun radiator in spring 1917, this machine served as a trainer with Flicks 37D and 50D until it crashed in January 1918.

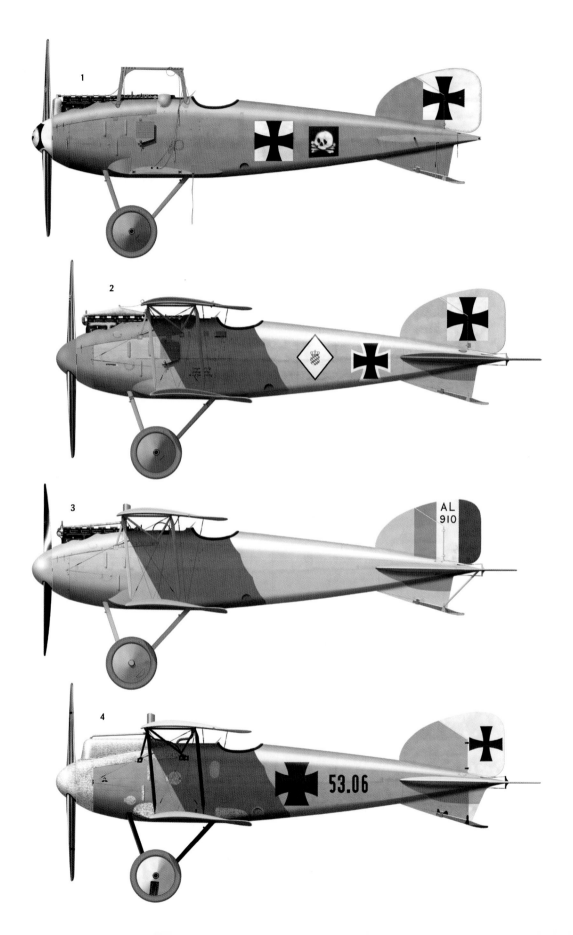

This line-up of Jasta 16b Albatros D.II (LVG)s exemplifies early versions of personal markings. As months passed, such markings would become more flamboyant and spread to cohesive colours and markings for entire Staffeln.

proved that colouring the fuselage (plywood parts) is possible without an appreciable increase in the A.U. weight (50 grams)'.

Ostdeutsche Albatros Werke (D.II 890–939/16)

OAW-built Albatros D.IIs were finished similarly to their Johannisthal brethren, with warm straw-yellow fuselage, grey or greyish-beige metal fittings, and with the wings and horizontal stabilizers/elevator finished in what has been described as 'patches of burnt sienna and light and dark green blending into one another' (although photographs reveal this 'blending' was often very course and rough) with 'undersurfaces very pale blue'. However, other OAW machines had their fuselages entirely camouflaged in the same manner and colours as the wings, including the course blending, with their bellies light blue from nose cowl to tailskid; engine panels remained a shade of grey. Eisernkreuz national markings were located at the usual eight points, all of which bore a 5cm white border instead of a square crossfield, although upper wing crosses were centred atop the interplane struts, and fuselage crosses were located further forward than those on the Johannisthal machines. Serial numbers were allocated to the wheel covers (which employed an oval rather than rectangular valve access hatch) instead of the vertical stabilizer, and the fuselage manufacture and Idflieg placards were located just below the cockpit.

Other visual OAW hallmarks included a ridge along the lower edges of the engine cowl panels, and what are believed to have been strips of fabric along the upper and lower longerons that covered engine ground wires routed aft.

Luftverkehrsgesellschaft (D.II 1024–1098/16)

LVG-built D.IIs shared the Albatros Flugzeugwerke machine's warm straw-yellow fuselage with the standard greyish metal fittings; wing root fairings were often wood. Wings, horizontal stabilizer, and elevator camouflage was distinctive in its appearance, with light and dark bands of burnt sienna, dark green and light Brunswick green that were diagonally mirrored on either side of the centreline. Wing undersurfaces have been described as 'pale greenish-blue' or 'duck-egg green', and the rudder was normally one of the uppersurface camouflage colours. National markings were in the usual eight-point positions, initially on white crossfields, later replaced by white-bordered crosses, although some machines displayed both types. Regardless, all wing crosses were centred slightly inboard of the interplane struts. Serial numbers were not seen on the vertical stabilizers and a three-line weights table was printed in black on the port fuselage, just above the wing.

Oesterreichische Flugzeugfabrik Allgemeine Gesellschaft (53.01–53.16)

Along with German manufacture, 16 Albatros D.IIs were produced by Oeffag of Wiener Neustadt, Austria. These machines were numbered 53.01 to 53.16. Austria designated the number '5' to Oeffag; '3' was the designation for Albatros; and the numbers right of the decimal point denoted the individual machines of the series.

Overall they employed the same semi-monocoque wooden construction as the German machines, with the spinner, cowl panels, and access hatches in bare, engine-turned metal. The wings, horizontal stabilizers, and all control surfaces were covered in clear-doped fabric. Eisernkreuz national markings were in the usual eight positions, but were slightly different from German markings. Wing crosses were without white borders or crossfields and placed fully inboard the interplane struts, while the rudder cross was also borderless and positioned entirely upon the rudder. Fuselage crosses were positioned similarly to those of OAW-built Albatros D.IIs, and appeared to have had white borders on early machines (as seen on 53.01 and 53.03) that were later painted black to create solid black crosses of beefier dimensions than those of the wings and rudder. Black serial numbers were painted aft of the fuselage cross in large, prominent numerals.

Staffel Finishes

The D.I and D.II's autumnal arrival in 1916 coincided with the formation of the Jagstaffeln (fighter or hunting squadrons). Generally they were not overpainted in the garish markings common by mid-1917. However, various Staffeln did employ unit markings, such as Jasta 23's swastika, while others based their markings on a 'theme', such as Jasta 2's abbreviated pilot names (although Ltn Manfred von Richthofen and Oblt Stefan Kirmaier preferred vertical stripes, and Staffelführer Hptm Oswald Boelcke used nothing at all). Jasta 5 used individual letters and numbers, and Kampfstaffel 11 preferred geometric symbols. Individual markings were not unknown, such as Jasta 22 pilot Josef Jacobs' 'Kobe' or Prince Friedrich Karl's skull and crossbones, inspired by his prior service with the 'Death's Head Hussars', 1.Leib-Husarem-Regiment Nr. 1. Partial or entire fuselage overpainting was not unknown either; several Jasta 2 machines were overpainted green or brown (including that flown by the Prince and Richthofen), although this practice also was neither as common nor as ostentatiously employed as would be seen during the following year. On the Eastern Front, Oeffag D.IIs retained their factory appearances.

Albatros D.I and D.II Technical Specifications

Manufacturer	Johannisthal	Johannisthal	Oeffag
Albatros	D.I	D.II	D.II(Oef)
Engine	160ps Mercedes D.III	160ps Mercedes D.III	185ps Daimler
Wingspan (upper)	8.5m (27ft 11in)	8.5m (27ft 11in)	8.5m (27ft 11in)
Wingspan (lower)	8m (26ft 3in)	8m (26ft 3in)	8m (26ft 3in)
Chord (upper wing)	1.6m (5ft 3in)	1.6m (5ft 3in)	1.7m (5ft 7in)
Chord (lower wing)	1.6m (5ft 3in)	1.6m (5ft 3in)	1.7m (5ft 7in)
Dihedral	none	none	none upper; 1° lower
Length	7.4m (24ft 3in)	7.4m (24ft 3in)	7.4m (24ft 3in)
Height	2.95m (9ft 8in)	2.64m (8ft 8in)	2.7m (8ft 10in)
Armament	2 x IMG 08/15 7.92mm MG	2 x IMG 08/15 7.92mm MG	1 or 2 M07/12 8.0mm MG
Weight (lb)			
Empty	1,530	1,484	1,521
Useful Load	502	D496	591
Loaded	109	109	106
Climb to			
1,000m (3,281 ft)	4 min	4 min	4 min–4 min 30 sec
2,000m (6,562 ft)	10 min	10 min	7–10 min
3,000m (9,843 ft)	19 min	19 min	12 min 30 sec–19 min
4,000m (13,123 ft)	30 min	30 min	–

24 Sqn DH2s 6000 (left) and 5925 (right) at Bertangles, July 1916. Two months later the DH.2 became the Albatros D.I's and D.II's principal single-seat adversary as the types clashed through autumn and into winter.

OPERATIONAL HISTORY

Despite the single-seat biplane production orders that Halberstadt and Albatros procured earlier in the year, in August 1916 the Fokker and Pfalz monoplanes still comprised the backbone of the Fliegertruppe's (Flying Corps) single-seat fighter contingency. But the success they had enjoyed since mid-1915 had been doomed by the arrival of the French Nieuport and British DH.2 fighters that drove the German monoplanes back on their heels; the 'Fokker Scourge' was over.

A portent of things to come had arrived on 25 April, when 24 Sqn DH.2s escorting B.E.2cs from 15 Sqn were attacked by a flight of Fokker Eindeckers, one of which was piloted by the great German ace Oblt Max Immelmann. Born on 21 September 1890, Immelmann joined the 2nd Railway Regiment

E **JASTA 2, 17 SEPTEMBER 1916**

On 17 September 1916 Jasta 2 Staffelführer Hptm Oswald Boelcke led several of his neophyte fighter pilots aloft in new Albatros D.I fighters, intercepting 11 Sqn F.E.2bs escorting bomb-laden B.E.2cs and providing the opportunity for future 'Red Baron' Ltn Manfred von Richthofen to attain his first credited aerial victory. 'The Englishman near me was a big, dark-coloured barge', as Richthofen later described F.E.2b 7018, crewed by pilot 2Lt Lionel Morris and observer Lt Tom Rees. 'I did not ponder long and took aim at him. He shot and I shot, but we both missed. The fight then began.' Morris manoeuvred the F.E.2 out of Richthofen's line of fire and continually upset the determined yet inexperienced pilot's aim, but then returned to straight and level flight. Richthofen opined the F.E.2 had lost visual contact. 'In a fraction of a second I was sitting on his tail. I gave him a short burst from my machine gun [sic – the Albatros D.I had two machine guns]... Then, suddenly, his propeller turned no more. Hit!' This scene depicts the dramatic moment immediately afterwards, as 7018 began its earthward glide. Although Richthofen is shown flying Albatros D.I 390/16, later associated with Jasta 2 pilot Ltn d R Otto Höhne, on this day pilots had to share too few machines. Therefore the identity of Richthofen's D.I is unknown.

in 1911 but by November 1914 had applied for aviation transfer and was learning to fly at Johannisthal. After a stint flying LVG two-seaters with FFA (Feldflieger Abteilung or Field Aviation Unit) 62, he began flying the section's single-seat Eindeckers and soon established himself as an aggressive fighter pilot, shooting down a then-incredible eight aeroplanes by mid-January 1916 to win the Orden Pour le Mérite. On the prowl on 25 April for victory number 15, Immelmann spotted the British machines some 700 metres higher than him and attacked them despite his altitude disadvantage. However, proceedings did not develop as he had anticipated:

> I ... came up and attacked one. He seemed to heel over after a few shots, but unfortunately I was mistaken. The two [enemy planes] worked splendidly together in the course of the fight and put 11 shots in my machine. The petrol tank, the struts on the fuselage, the undercarriage and the propeller were hit. I could only save myself by a nose-dive of 1,000 metres.

These bedeviling DH.2s were flown by Lt N. P. Manfield and 2Lt John Oliver Andrews (the latter of whom would be involved in one of the war's most legendary aerial battles in the coming autumn). The result of their actions against Immelmann, who was killed less than two months later on 18 June fighting 25 Sqn F.E.2bs, supplied an enormous confidence boost to the pilots of 24 Sqn; they had met the dreaded Fokker and the Fokker had been theirs. They never looked back.

Later that summer, on 21 July, a 24 Sqn DH.2 patrol happened upon several LFG Roland C.II Walfisch near Roisel, escorted by Fokker Eindeckers. During the subsequent combat Andrews shot down an Eindecker that he saw execute a hard forced landing that sheared off its undercarriage, after which Andrews dived down and strafed a group of Germans approaching the fallen machine.

It is believed that this first of Andrews' 12 victories was eight-victory ace and Orden Pour le Mérite winner Ltn Otto Parschau, commander of Abwehrkommando Nord (Defence Command North, or AKN). Born on 11 November 1890 in East Prussia, Parschau served in the 151st Infantry Regiment and then learned to fly in 1913, receiving his pilot certificate that July. After the war began the following year, he flew with FFA 42, FFA 261, and Brieftauben-Abteilung-Ostende (Carrier Pigeon Section, or BAO), and was credited with downing six two-seaters and two observation balloons by 9 July 1916. Mortally wounded during the action of 21 July, he managed to reach earth safely and receive medical attention, but died of his wounds during an operation that evening.

Although credited to Andrews flying DH.2 5948, the precise time of Parschau's downing is unknown and creates uncertainty regarding the identity of his victor; some suggest it may have been the celebrated and colourful French ace Ltn Charles Nungesser. In any event, the East Prussian's death was the second to befall an Orden Pour le Mérite-decorated aviator (Immelmann being the first). As Greg VanWyngarden wrote in Osprey's *Early German Aces of World War 1*, 'Parschau's death placed another exclamation point on the end of any semblance of German control of the air over the Somme.'

Help finally arrived with the appearance of the first Halberstadt D.II and D.III biplane fighters, which began trickling to the Western Front in late June. These machines were well received and praised for their excellent overall performance and handling characteristics, as future Orden Pour le Mérite winner and 44-victory ace Ltn Josef Jacobs noted while flight instructing at Jastaschule 1: 'During the afternoon I took up a Halberstadt for the first time. The machine was extraordinarily easy to fly, was very fast and stable, and possessed no vices.' Pilots would have preferred that the Halberstadt had two machine guns rather than just one, but still it was a marked improvement over the various Eindeckers. However, there just were not enough of them. By 31 August the front-line inventory contained only 25 Halberstadt D-types (five D.IIs and 20 D.IIIs), and these few machines were scattered in twos and threes about the various units. Despite their low numbers, Idflieg's writing was on the wall for the monoplanes:

> Equipping the field squadrons with four E-type monoplanes each is almost complete. The performance of this type, after installation of a second machine gun and a 160Ps rotary engine [Fokker E IV], has reached its zenith. The D-type biplane fighter which came to the Front several weeks ago, has proved superior not only with respect to speed and rate of climb but also in manoeuvrability. It will replace the E-type; the conversion has begun.

There had also been a reorganization within the Fliegertruppe, as the first Jagdstaffeln were formed using the pilots and aeroplanes of the Kampfeinsitzer Kommandos (single-seat fighter detachments, or KEK). The Jastas were developed so that each employed 14 new D-type fighters on a two-fold mission. First, they were to seek and destroy enemy fighters to protect German army cooperation two-seater reconnaissance aeroplanes from interruption and molestation; second, they were to seek and destroy enemy two-seater reconnaissance and artillery-spotting aeroplanes.

At the in-field forefront of this reorganization was the Orden Pour le Mérite-decorated Hptm Oswald Boelcke, Germany's leading ace with 19 victories. Born on 19 May 1891 in the Halle suburb of Giebichenstein in Saxony, Boelcke was the fourth child of a high school professor. The family moved to Dessau, where Boelcke graduated from the Friedrichs Gymnasium in 1911, after which he served in the Prussian Cadet Corps Telegrapher's Battalion until an interest in aviation led him to transfer into the Fliegertruppe and become a pilot in 1914. When World War I began that August, Boelcke served with FA 13 (Flieger Abteilung 13, or Flying Unit/Section 13) and flew two-seaters with his brother Wilhelm as observer, and by

Jasta 2 Staffelführer Hptm Oswald Boelcke. The Orden Pour le Mérite-decorated, 40-victory ace combined his experienced fighter tactics and training with the new Albatros D.I and D.II to reap considerable success for Jasta 2 in autumn 1916. Boelcke shot down 14 aeroplanes in six weeks while flying an Albatros.

Hauptmann Boelcke. †

363
Postkartenvertrieb W.S
BERLIN N. 37.
Nachdruck wird gerichtlich

Jasta 2 Albatros D.Is lined up at Lagnicourt, early autumn 1916. The machine at far right with the nose expansion tank and Axial propeller was likely later painted green and flown by Ltn d R Diether Collin and Prussian Prinz Friedrich Karl. Karl was flying the machine on 21 March 1917 when wounded by a 32 Sqn DH.2 and forced to land between the lines, after which he was shot in the spine and killed while fleeing towards German territory. His D.I was captured and assigned the RFC identification G-17.

February 1915 he had received the Iron Cross First and Second classes. Flying an LVG C I with FFA 62, Boelcke and his new observer scored a victory over a Morane Parasol, and thereafter he was driven by an interest in aerial combat that led to flying single-seat Fokker Eindeckers. Via this new form of warfare he shot down several more aeroplanes in autumn 1915 as part of the infamous 'Fokker Scourge', and for this achievement he received the Orden Pour le Mérite on 12 January 1916.

Upon the death of FFA 62 comrade and rival Max Immelmann that June, Boelcke was grounded and given the choice of a desk job or an 'inspection tour' of the Balkans, lest he too be killed and national morale further damaged. He chose the latter. Prior to his departure, he visited the Feldflugchef (Aviation Chief of Staff) and discussed the need for permanent single-seater units (ultimately realized with the formation of the Jagdstaffeln), suggested that pilots should adhere to strict formation flying, and shared his principles for aerial combat. Known as 'Dicta Boelcke', these principles stressed minimum personal risk and maximum tactical advantage:

F JASTA 2, 27 SEPTEMBER 1916

A week after Jasta 2 received its first Albatros D.Is and Boelcke's pre-production D.II, British artillery and aerial bombing forced the Staffel to abandon its Bertincourt aerodrome for one a few miles further behind the lines, near Lagnicourt. Boelcke suffered asthma-related ill health during this move, but by the 27th was well back in action, attacking an outclassed Martinsyde G 100 of 27 Sqn flown by 2Lt Henry Taylor. 'I gave the signal to attack', Boelcke wrote, 'and a general battle started. I attacked one; got too close; ducked under him and, turning, saw an Englishman fall like a plummet'. Taylor was killed and Boelcke credited with his 29th overall victory, his third flying the new Albatros D.II. Boelcke attained a further 11 credited victories behind the guns of 386/16 until a collision in combat-congested airspace led to the legendary airman's death.

1. Try to secure advantages before attacking. If possible keep the sun behind you.

2. Always carry through an attack when you have started it.

3. Fire only at close range and only when your opponent is properly in your sights.

4. Always keep your eye on your opponent, and never let yourself be deceived by ruses.

5. In any form of attack it is essential to assail your opponent from behind.

6. If your opponent dives on you, do not try to evade his onslaught, but fly to meet it.

7. When over the enemy's lines never forget your own line of retreat.

8. For the Staffel: Attack on principle in groups of four or six. When the fight breaks up into a series of single combats, take care that several do not go for one opponent.

The tattered remains of 24 Sqn Ltn P. A. Langan-Byrne's DH.2 A2542, shot down on 16 October 1916 by Oswald Boelcke for his 34th victory.

During his inspection tour, the British Somme offensive had begun, and in August Boelcke was recalled to the Western Front and tasked with assembling the second Jagdstaffel, Jasta 2. At least partly comprised of eager single-seat fighter neophytes that Boelcke selected from various two-seater units, Jasta 2 had formed approximately three weeks before its share of new Albatros D.Is and D.IIs became available. Thus Boelcke flew 'lone wolf' patrols with a rotary-engined Fokker D.III and shot down eight more aeroplanes until the new Albatros Ds began arriving on 16 September.

And none too soon. During the first two weeks of the Staffel's existence only a single Albatros D.I from neighbouring Jasta 1 had arrived to join a ragtag collection of one Fokker D.I, one Fokker D.III, and one 'refurbished' Halberstadt D-type. This meant there were only three machines to be shared amongst the Staffel while Boelcke flew the Fokker D.III, so the pilots' time-in-air was limited, particularly with the sole Albatros D.I. When the five new pre-production D.Is and single D.II for Boelcke (with the Teeves and Braun wing radiator rather than the D.I's fuselage-mounted Windhoffs) arrived, they still left the Staffel short of machines, but at least they signified an end to the drought. This was just in time, as, according to Boelcke: 'My pilots are all passionately keen and very competent, but I must first train them to steady teamwork – they are at present rather like young puppies in their zeal to achieve something.'

None of these 'young puppies' had more than a few hours, if that, in an Albatros D-type, but on 17 September Boelcke led them and their new machines on a late-morning sortie toward the lines. Inside one D.I was former two-seater pilot Ltn Manfred von Richthofen. Known worldwide today as 'The Red Baron', on that autumn morning Richthofen was a neophyte fighter pilot who the previous month had been among those selected by Boelcke to join the newly-formed Jasta 2. Born on 2 May 1892 in Breslau, Silesia, Germany, Richthofen entered military academy in 1909 and upon graduation was assigned to the 1st Uhlan Regiment. When war began he served on the Eastern and Western Fronts but became bored with trench warfare and transferred into the Fliegertruppe as an observer, serving several months in that capacity until learning to fly and attaining his pilot certificate on Christmas Day 1915. He then flew two-seater reconnaissance and bombing sorties on both Fronts, but driven by a desire to fly single-seat fighters he rigged a machine gun to an LFG Roland C.II and shot down a Nieuport scout, although this victory was not officially confirmed.

Armed with at least this small taste of aerial combat when following Boelcke on 17 September, Richthofen detected 'shrapnel clouds' (anti-aircraft fire) over the Front and spotted several aeroplanes flying towards Cambrai. These were bomb-laden 12 Sqn B.E.2ds escorted by 11 Sqn F.E.2bs, inbound on a sortie against Marcoing station. After Boelcke led his men behind the RFC machines to cut off their retreat, Richthofen went after F.E.2b 7018, crewed by pilot 2Lt Lionel Morris and observer Lt Tom Rees. Approaching the 'darkly painted barge' from low and behind, he 'did not ponder long and took aim at him. He shot and I shot, but we both missed. The fight then began.' Endeavouring to remain in the manoeuvring pusher's blind spot as he traded bursts with Rees, Richthofen later noted that he had not the 'conviction I have now that ¡he must fall,¡ but, rather, I was much more anxious to see *if* he would fall'.

It has been said that neophyte pilots have an empty bag of experience and a full bag of luck, and one needs to fill the former before emptying the latter.

Oswald Boelcke wipes his face post-sortie next to Albatros D.II 386/16, Lagnicourt, autumn 1916. This photo affords a clear view of the swirls seen on wings and rudders of several pre-production Albatros C and D types, of which this was one. Note the rudder bellcrank access hatch on the tail, and that the upper wing crossfield was not full chord.

Richthofen was no exception, for he concentrated so intently on the task before him that he experienced target fixation and confessed afterwards that 'it did not occur to me that there were other Englishman in the squadron who could come to the aid of their hard-pressed comrade. There was only the growing thought: ìHe must fall, come what may!' Fortunately, this mythical bag of luck held and he was not attacked by another F.E.2 as he closed to within ten metres of 7018's tail, firing several bursts until 'the enemy propeller stood stock still', forcing the aeroplane into a gliding descent.

Recalling the moment in his 1917 autobiography *Der Rote Kampfflieger* (The Red Battle Flyer), Richthofen wrote that when 7018 began its gliding descent he 'noticed the machine swaying from side to side' and opined 'something was not quite right with the pilot.' Indeed, it is possible that Morris had been wounded to some extent. Richthofen's autobiography also states 'the observer was not to be seen, his machine gun pointed unattended up in the air ... I had no doubt hit him also, and he must have been lying on the floor of the fuselage'. It is likely this recollection was abridged, because his combat report states 'the machine went down gliding and I followed until I had killed the observer who had not stopped shooting until the last moment', at which point 7018 'went downwards in sharp curves'. This suggests that Richthofen actually killed Rees during one of his continued attacks against the gliding machine, not when he shot up 7018's engine, and since this was when the FE2 entered a spiralling descent it is possible that this was when Morris was wounded, or perhaps wounded more seriously. In any event, it mattered little; the mortally wounded Morris managed to land the stricken pusher but followed Rees into eternity shortly thereafter. Richthofen's first credited victory was the first of 12 F.E.2s he eventually shot down, five while flying an Albatros D.I or D.II.

Nearby, Boelcke had also scored, shooting up the engine of an F.E.2b from the 'rear and underneath' where the F.E.2s' return fire could not reach (as he had taught Richthofen), and forcing the FE2 to glide down to a dead-stick landing near Equancourt, where the crew burned the machine before being captured. Boelcke wrote that he usually strove to attack 'at an angle from behind [because] to get him [the enemy] from directly behind is not so good, since the motor acts as a protection', suggesting his primary aiming point was the crew.

Ltn Erwin Böhme had scored the day's first victory earlier that morning, shooting down 70 Sqn Sopwith 1½ Strutter A1913 northwest of Hervilly at 0745 hours. The pilot 2Lt Oswald Nixon was killed and observer 2Lt Ronald Wood was wounded, 'shot unconscious' for two weeks and never able to recall the details of his downing. By the end of October Böhme had five confirmed victories (one Nieuport XII, two 1½ Strutters, two F.E.2bs) and one unconfirmed victory (a Martinsyde G 100) and had the utmost confidence in his Albatros D.I:

Our new aircraft border likewise on marvellous. Compared to the single-seater which we flew before Verdun [the Fokker Eindecker], they are improved. Their rate of climb and turning radius are amazing. It is as if they are living, feeling creatures that understand what the pilot wishes. With them one may risk everything and succeed.

[Dogfighting] would be unthinkable in the heavy two-seaters. However, with our light single-seaters, the pilot is in a completely different situation. It is, if I may say, a personal unity with the machine. One no longer has the feeling that he is sitting in and flying an airplane, but it is as if there were a spiritual interaction. It is similar to a good horseman who is not only letting the horse carry him and is attempting through various commands to communicate to the horse his intentions, but who has grown so completely together with his horse, that the horse immediately feels what the rider wants. Both have total understanding of and trust in one another, and they are

Jasta 6 pilot Vzfw Carl Holler smiles from within an OAW-built Albatros D.II. Other photos reveal this machine had a light/dark camouflaged fuselage with pale blue undersides and a dark '9' within a white vertical rectangle, just forward of the fuselage Eisernkreuz. Note the mirror, covered radiator, manufacture placards, and taped longeron.

motivated with one will. I can only compare the true joy of a horseman with the bliss I feel in being completely one with my Albatros.

Thereafter Jasta 2 flew multi-plane patrols, the presence and impact of which were noted immediately by the RFC. As per their purpose, Jasta 2 preyed upon many B.E.2c, Sopwith 1½ Strutter and F.E.2b two-seaters, but inevitably the Albatros D.I and D.II and Airco DH.2 found themselves fighting as well.

The early contacts were stalemates, such as on 15 September when three DH.2s from 24 Sqn attacked 2 HA approaching our lines from the Bapaume–Peronne road. One machine went down vertically for 1,000 feet then side-slipped and flattened out. A small single-seater scout continually attacked, and owing to its superior speed and climb, could not be continually engaged.

Soon the encounters became bloodier, such as on 16 October when Boelcke attacked a 24 Sqn DH.2 flown by 'C' Flight commander and ten-victory ace Lt P. A. Langan-Byrne, on offensive patrol with several other DH.2s. Boelcke wrote that at 1745 hours he spotted the 'C' Flight pushers:

[I] went into some fine turns. The English leader, with streamers on his machine, came just right for me. I settled him with my first attack – apparently the pilot was killed, for the machine spun down. I watched it down until it crashed about a kilometre east of Beaulencourt.

It was his 34th total victory and his 15th victory since Jasta 2's formation six weeks previously.

Eight of these victories had been attained behind the guns of pre-production Albatros D.II 386/16. On 19 September he shot down a 60 Sqn Morane despite enduring a jammed machine gun, an obvious boon of having two independently firing weapons; on 7 October he shot down a Nieuport XII that he had 'attacked from twenty or thirty metres behind' and 'pounded him till he exploded with a great yellow flare'; and ten days later he forced down an 11 Sqn F.E.2 to low altitude where he shot it down in flames 'after the second volley'.

Jasta 2 Staffelführer Oblt Stefan Kirmaier stands before Albatros D.II 4--/16 at Lagnicourt, very late October or November 1916. Note feathered pale blue undersurface demarcation, identification streamers on the interplane struts, and upper wing crossfields that extend to the leading edge. Shiny tyres indicate the field was wet when the D.II was rolled into position.

As a whole the Staffel attained 51 credited victories between 2 September and 26 October 1916, with Boelcke downing 21 aeroplanes to reach 40 total victories. Oblt Stefan Kirmaier attained his seventh total victory, and future Orden Pour le Mérite winners Richthofen, Böhme, and OfStv Max Müller reached 6, 5, and 2 total victories respectively. DH2 pilot 2Lt Gwilym H. Lewis of 32 Sqn wrote on 23 October:

> The good days of July and August, when two or three DHs used to push half-a-dozen Huns onto the chimney tops of Bapaume, are no more. In the Roland they possessed the finest two-seater machine in the world, and now they have introduced a few of their single-seater ideas, and very good they are too, one specimen especially deserves mention. They are manned by jolly good pilots, probably the best, and the juggling they can do when they are scrapping is quite remarkable. They can fly round and round a DH and make one look quite silly.

By this time the first production Albatros D.IIs began arriving at the Jagdstaffeln, intermingling with the D.Is already present. Flying these new machines under Boelcke's skill and leadership had a profound effect on the Staffel. Its morale soared. 'It is somewhat unique how Boelcke conveys his spirit to each and every one of his students, how he carries them all away', wrote Böhme. 'They follow him wherever he leads. Not one would leave him in the lurch! He is a born leader! No wonder that his *Staffel* blossoms!' Future 80-victory ace and Orden Pour le Mérite-decorated Manfred von Richthofen had similar sentiments, writing retrospectively:

> It was a wonderful time at our squadron. The spirit of the leader spread to his pupils. We could blindly trust his leadership. There was no possibility that anyone would be left behind. The thought never came to us. And so we roamed bright and merry, diminishing our enemies.

As fine and successful as these new fighters were, they were not invulnerable; invariably, there were losses. On 30 September Jasta 2's Ltn Ernst Diener was

Manfred von Richthofen and a photographer stand before a Jasta 2 Albatros D.II – the same machine with which he appeared earlier – and several D.Is. The absence of fuselage crossfields suggests all were overpainted in dark colours. The D.II and far right D.I certainly were, indicated by dark engine cowls and altered/covered tail crossfields.

shot down by a Nieuport scout believed flown by 12-victory French ace S/Lt René Dorme of Escadrille N.3, and the next day Ltn Herwarth Philipps was shot down, beaten by anti-aircraft fire or 32 Sqn DH.2s. Even Boelcke was not invincible, noting that on 10 October he pursued a 'Vickers' machine but 'by skilful flying, he escaped'. It was to get worse.

On Saturday 28 October, Boelcke and Staffelkamerad and personal friend Böhme had just sat down to enjoy a game of chess when Jasta 2 'were called shortly after four o'clock during an infantry attack on the front'. Boelcke had flown several sorties already that day, but led his Staffel of Albatros D.Is and D.IIs aloft again into cloudy, stormy skies. Richthofen accompanied the flight and recalled that while flying at about 10,000 feet between Pozières and Flers, 'from a great distance we saw two imprudent Englishmen over the Front, apparently having fun in the bad weather.' These two aeroplanes were 24 Sqn 'C' Flight DH.2s flown by six-victory ace Ltn Arthur Gerald Knight (DH.2 A2594) and Ltn Alfred Edwin McKay (DH.2 A2554) flying a NE–SW defensive patrol between Pozières and Bapaume. At 8,500 feet, Knight was about 1,500 feet higher than McKay, whose departure from Bertangles had been delayed 'on account of [a] dud engine', forcing him to take a second machine aloft that he noted 'would not climb'; typical examples of engine woes often faced by 24 Sqn. At about 1640 hours the pair spotted Jasta 2's Albatrosses and identified them as 'Halberstadters and small Aviatic [sic] Scouts' who stalked them for five minutes until one 'did a side-slipping dive under the top D.H., but Lieut. Knight did not attack as he was suspicious of this manoeuvre'.

As the leader, it is likely that this attacking aeroplane was Boelcke, who according to Richthofen 'went after one and I the other'. Knight wrote that he was initially attacked by six of the 12 aeroplanes and immediately commenced evasive spiralling before the other six attacked, some of whom went down below him and attacked McKay as well. Outnumbered six-to-one, the DH.2s could do little amidst the swirling cloud of German fighters. 'It would have been fatal to concentrate on any one machine as four or five [others] were ready to close in,' wrote Knight, 'so I merely spiralled and fired when a HA [Hostile Aircraft] came across my sights.'

The same opinion was had by Böhme, who in a letter to his fiancée wrote that 'the English aircraft, fast single-seaters, skilfully defended themselves' during a 'wildly gyrating mêlée in which we could always only get into range for brief moments.' No doubt the sheer number of German aeroplanes chasing the same two targets crowded the airspace, aiding the British and threatening to violate Boelcke's eighth dictum that cautioned against several fighters pursuing the same opponent, although perhaps there was little choice in so lopsided a battle. Regardless, the threat proved all too real. After 'about five minutes of strenuous fighting' during which Jasta 2 'attempted to force our opponents downward by alternately blocking their path, as we had previously so often done with success', Boelcke and Böhme were pursuing McKay when Knight, under attack by Richthofen, turned hard left to evade and cut in front of McKay's pursuers. Both Germans manoeuvred to avoid colliding with the DH.2, but tragically collided with each other instead, each Albatros having been in the blind spot of the other. Böhme's undercarriage struck Boelcke's upper port wing; the impact was described as a 'light touch', but Böhme lost a portion of his undercarriage and the outboard section of Boelcke's wing was torn away. 'How can I describe my feelings from that moment on,' Böhme later wrote, 'when Boelcke suddenly appeared just a few metres to my right, how he dived, how I jerked upward [after each had become aware of their too-close proximity], and how we nevertheless grazed each other, and both plummeted downward!'

Böhme fell a couple of hundred metres but recovered to follow Boelcke's crippled D.II, gliding left-wing-low 'in great spiralling curves' toward the clouds. His description of this descent suggests that Boelcke had also lost his port aileron, which would reduce or eliminate use of the starboard aileron, or, if the starboard aileron still functioned, it was not enough fully to arrest the roll caused by the now asymmetrical lift created by the partly missing wing. Richthofen wrote that he followed Boelcke as well, at least initially, and his account agreed with Böhme's that Boelcke descended from the fight while under some control. Knight and McKay also saw Boelcke's initial decent and concurred his Albatros was under control. However, he entered a lower layer of clouds (in which one encounters increased turbulence) and thence, according to Richthofen, lost his entire upper wing. Böhme observed that Boelcke 'went into an ever steepening glide, and I saw before the landing how he could no longer keep his plane facing straightforward, and how he struck the ground near a gun battery.'

Böhme attempted to land nearby but was thwarted by the surrounding shell holes and trenches and was forced to return to Jasta 2's base at Lagnicourt. His damaged Albatros undercarriage caused him to nose over on landing; unhurt, he and several others drove back to the crash site with hopes of Boelcke's survival, but these were dashed by the grim reality of Boelcke's corpse that the adjacent gun crew had extricated from the wreckage. Böhme opined the crash might have been survivable had Boelcke worn a crash helmet (something not usually done by Jagdstaffelpiloten) and had strapped himself firmly into his D.II, which might have better protected him from the blunt-force trauma that had fractured his skull and killed him. In any event, the great 40-victory ace was dead. That night, Boelcke's brother Wilhelm sent a telegram to their sister: 'Prepare parents: Oswald mortally injured today over German lines.'

Meanwhile, McKay and Knight continued their swirling battle above against the rest of Jasta 2 for another 15 minutes after the collision, each DH.2 having descended to 5,000 feet and drifting east of Bapaume. Finally, the Albatros scouts disengaged to the east and the DH.2s returned to

Diether Collin's (hence 'CO') Albatros D.I prior to being taken aloft by Prince Karl, suiting up at left. Seen earlier in a Jasta 2 line-up, the machine is now painted green except for rudder and fuselage/tail crossfields, although upper wing crossfields are overpainted. Note the anemometer mounted to the forward starboard interplane strut. The device on the lower wing is a makeshift platform set upon the fore and aft standing points. This D.I is often misidentified as 384/16, but that machine had larger crosses, untouched upper wing crossfields, a Reschke propeller, and horizontal stabilizer struts, and appeared as such when destroyed in a crash.

Bertangles, where they landed safely at 1740 hours. By the time Jasta 2 returned en masse to Lagnicourt, word of Boelcke's death had already reached the aerodrome. Naturally, the pilots were shocked. 'One could hardly conceive of it', recalled Richthofen.

Aerial combat was not a fighter pilot's only hazard. Many sorties did not even involve combat, and those that did contained only a fractionally small few minutes of such mortal danger. Mostly, a fighter pilot *flew*, and even in new and reliable machines such as an Albatros D.II a pilot could encounter a myriad of unexpected problems that caused or led to emergency situations. Jasta 6 pilot Vzfw Carl Holler experienced one such event the day after receiving the new Albatros D.II 484/16:

> I started at 0806 hours as the third machine of the First Kette [with] orders to provide high-flying cover for the attack on Pressoir Wood by refusing enemy recce flights entrance to the Front... After termination of our patrol time, my Kettenführer signalled me to fly home, at which we started a glide downwards from 4,300 metres. After a few moments, I lost my leader due to oil-dirtied goggles. On removing them, I got oil in my eyes, which made flying very difficult. I flew [through] the low clouds which were as low as 60 metres. Near an unknown village (which I overflew thrice), I chose a meadow to force land on. I landed and rolled towards a road with trees. I stopped the engine and on inspection noted that the oil pipe had broken, so the oil was pumping into my face. I removed the fuel from the emergency tank to the main tank, and fixed the oil pipe. While cleaning my goggles, I noticed French soldiers approaching my machine. So, I had landed on the wrong side! Luckily my engine had kept its compression and I started at once, first turning from the trees amidst a volley of gunfire that only stopped when I disappeared into the clouds. Now I flew due east, but after 25 minutes I had to land again because my improvization went wrong and the oiling started anew. Now I was over our own territory, near Hamm sur Somme. I started again but had to land a third time because of fog over my airfield. I now [diverted] to Ennemain [after which] at 11.40 hours I at last reached my base.

Despite these problems Holler praised the new Albatros D machines, noting that

> [the D.I's] rate of climb was excellent – it was child's play to reach 5,000 metres. Because of its heavy in-line engine, it had a tremendous diving speed, which gave us great advantage when attacking the enemy flying below. Now we did not have to wait long to obtain victories.

On 30 October 1916, seven-victory ace Oblt Stefan Kirmaier was appointed Staffelführer of Jasta 2. Born 28 July 1889 at Lachen, Kirmaier served with the 8th Infantry Regiment until his transfer into the Fliegertruppe, where he flew with FA(A)203 in 1915–16 before his attachment to KEK Jametz, with whom he scored three victories. Joining Jasta 2 in early October, Kirmaier served under Boelcke and downed another four aeroplanes prior to his assumption of command.

On 13 November the last thrust of the Somme offensive began with the Battle of the Ancre. Four days later Kirmaier led Jasta 2 in a clash with their RFC rivals 24 Sqn, which lost a DH.2 to Ltn Höhne's guns, killing 2Lt W. C. Crawford. On 22 November, Kirmaier led Jasta 2 over the lines west of Bapaume, where they shot down a 3 Sqn Morane Parasol (Böhme's seventh victory) and an 11 Sqn F.E.2b (Ltn Erich König's second victory). However, several 24 Sqn DH.2s were in the area, many of whom saw the Parasol falling (which was able to regain the lines and limp home with a wounded crew). There are variations as to what transpired next, but according to the 24 Sqn Record Book, Capt Andrews (who had become temporary captain on 30 April) and Ltn K. Crawford reported 'several HA [Hostile Aircraft] dived' at them. Andrews claimed they did not fire at him and he was able to fasten on to the tail of the lowest machine and 'fired about ten rounds when he tried to jink and then fell out of control'. Meanwhile, Crawford wrote that after he 'got on one HA's tail and fired half a drum, he nosed dived', after which he 'saw Capt Andrews just above me' – ostensibly both men were attacking the same Albatros. Böhme's recollection of events was 'five of us were under way and we were attacked by two big squadrons at the same time over there. Each of us had to handle several opponents. I saw Kirmaier as he hotly pursued a Vickers two-seater, but had several behind him.'

Despite these account discrepancies, it was indeed Kirmaier who had attracted the attention of Andrews and Crawford, whose DH.2s now pursued the stricken Albatros into the thick ground mist below. Andrews continued firing until he lost sight of Kirmaier in the reduced visibility, but 'could follow the smoke trail made by his engine' and eventually discovered that the machine had crashed between Les Boeufs and Le Transloy. Crawford and Andrews circled 1,500 feet above the wreckage, but when they turned for home Crawford's 'engine conked' and he was forced to land 2,000 yards south of Guedecourt and 1,500 yards east of Flers. Securing his DH.2, Crawford met up with a major of the 3rd Australian Battery and walked back to the wreckage of Kirmaier's D.II:

> Found Hun machine at N.28a central. Pilot was killed shot through the back. Machine was a single-seater with ALBATROSS [sic] on his tail. The engine was buried beneath ground. He had 2 machine guns fixed one either side of his engine, each with a 500 round belt. These guns were taken by an officer of the 15th Australian Infantry Brigade, Gen Elliot, in a damaged condition.

Jasta 2 had lost their second Staffelführer in a month to 24 Sqn DH.2s. Non-pilot Oblt Karl Bodenschatz was appointed acting Staffelführer, but Richthofen was the de facto Staffelführer in the air. Flying in this capacity the next day, Richthofen spotted three 24 Sqn DH.2s led by Andrews, followed by Capt Robert Henry Magnus Spencer Saundby and 24 Sqn commanding officer Major Lanoe George Hawker, VC, DSO. Born on 30 December 1890 in Longparish, England, Hawker had flown reconnaissance sorties with 6 Sqn during the early war, and on 19 April 1915 he conducted a solo B.E.2c bombing mission against the Gontrode Zeppelin sheds near Ghent, Belgium, for which he won the Distinguished Service Order (DSO). As the war progressed, he flew reconnaissance sorties in F.E.2bs and later acquired a single-seat Bristol Scout that he rigged with a fuselage-mounted machine gun that fired obliquely outside the propeller arc. With this aeroplane, Hawker attacked and received credit for downing two Albatros C-type two-seaters on 25 July, one of which 'burst into flames and turned upside down, the observer falling out. The machine and pilot crashed to earth.' Hawker received the Victoria Cross (VC) for these two victories, the first RFC scout pilot so decorated. During the following month Hawker claimed three additional victories and returned to England in September to assume command of 24 Sqn, a weeks-old unit with which he spent the next four months training pilots on

Excellent post-capture view of Jasta 5 Albatros D.II (OAW) 910/16, seen here repainted aluminium with French markings and a Levasseur propeller. Captured by the RFC as G 14 March 1917, it was given to the French and designated AL 910. Note the OAW-style wing root fairing and oval tyre valve cover. Also, struts have been added to the horizontal stabilizer.

various two-seaters. Eventually re-equipped with DH.2s, the squadron departed for France and on 10 February established residence at Bertangles, whereupon 'war-flying proper immediately commenced'. Thereafter, Hawker's command responsibilities precluded his mission participation and eroded his combat currency, but nevertheless he made efforts to accompany his pilots whenever the pilot pool was low or there was a pilot about to go on leave.

Such was the case on 23 November, when at 1300 hours Hawker followed Andrews on an uneventful sortie until 1330 hours, when they spotted a 'rough house going on over Grandcourt' between 60 Sqn Nieuports and unidentified 'HA'. The DH.2s power-dived to join the fight, but arrived after the Nieuports had driven away most of the German airplanes, after which a DH.2 piloted by Ltn John Henry Crutch developed engine trouble enough to force a precautionary landing, leaving Andrews, Saundby, and Hawker to continue inbound without him. Shortly after 1350 hours, Andrews spotted two German two-seaters flying at 6,000 feet north-east of Bapaume and immediately led the trio into a diving attack that 'drove them [the Germans] east'. Yet during this chase Andrews discovered 'two strong patrols of H.A. scouts above me' and discontinued his pursuit in the face of such a threat, but reported that 'a D.H. Scout, [flown by] Maj. Hawker, dived past me and continued to pursue'. Not wanting to abandon Hawker – ostensibly unaware of the German scouts above him – Andrews and Saundby followed him eastward and 'were at once attacked by the H.A., one of which dived on to Maj. Hawker's tail'.

These attacking scouts were Richthofen's Albatros D.Is and D.IIs, which tore into the disadvantaged DH.2s and sent Saundby spiralling away 'two or three times' before the Germans disengaged and 'zoomed off'. Andrews went after an Albatros attacking Hawker and 'drove him off firing about 25 rounds at close range', but in the process was attacked by a fourth Albatros who shot up his engine until Saundby chased him away in a power-dive, enabling Andrews to glide across the lines without further molestation and to make a successful dead-stick landing in friendly territory. Unable to catch the diving

Albatros, Saundby pulled level and saw that the German aeroplanes had moved away to the east. Andrews was gliding nearby, but he saw no sign of Hawker. He then spotted Hawker 'at about 3,000 feet near Bapaume, fighting with an H.A. apparently quite under control but going down'.

This observation denotes the approximate midpoint of the now legendary combat between Hawker and Richthofen, which by Andrews' eyewitness account had developed into a continuous series of tight descending spirals. As Richthofen's *Der Rote Kampfflieger* described: 'Thus we both turned like madmen in circles, with engines running full-throttle at 3,500 metres height. First 20 times left, then 30 times right, each mindful of getting above and behind the other.' At 500 metres Hawker ceased spiralling and began evasive aerobatics that involved 'looping and such tricks', after which he broke for the lines in a zig-zagging descent from 100 metres. Richthofen pursued, firing steadily as his faster Albatros gained on the jinking DH.2, but at 30 metres altitude his guns jammed and 'almost cost me success'. Clearing his weapons, Richthofen resumed firing until 'fifty metres behind our lines' he saw Hawker's DH.2 begin an unchecked shallow descent and then hit the artillery-ravaged terrain near Ligny-Thilloy, one mile south of Bapaume. German soldiers later inspecting the wreck determined Hawker had been shot once in the back of the head. He was buried next to his destroyed aeroplane, but ultimately his grave was lost in the turmoil of war. (For a more complete account and analysis of this fight, see Osprey's Duel 42, *DH.2 vs Albatros D.I/D.II*.)

As Immelmann's death had symbolically signified the end of the 'Fokker Scourge' and German aerial supremacy, Hawker's death signified the reclamation of German aerial supremacy.

Four days later, Jasta 2 newcomer Leutnant der Reserve (Ltn d R) Werner Voss took off from Lagnicourt in search of his first victory. Voss was the future Orden Pour le Mérite-decorated, 48-victory ace, considered by many to be Germany's greatest World War I fighter pilot, beyond even Richthofen and Ernst Udet, the first and second highest scoring German pilots with 80 and

Flik 7D Albatros D.II (Oef) 53.16. Based on the raised tail, sunken wheels, and casual manner of those present, it appears the machine is receiving armament or synchronization servicing.

62 victories respectively. He gained his victory at 0940 hours, when flying an Albatros (whether a D.I or D.II is unclear) over Bapaume. He attacked a 60 Sqn Nieuport 17 flown by Capt George Aleck Parker DSO MC, whose aeroplane came down behind German lines near Miraumont. Parker's body was never recovered. Later that afternoon, Jasta 2 was in the air again and encountered several 18 Sqn F.E.2bs patrolling the Front. Voss attacked machine number 4915, crewed by pilot Lt Frederic Ambrose George and Observer 1/A.M. Oliver Frank Watts. According to the RFC Combat Casualties report for 27 November, 4915 was 'brought down in flames. Pilot wounded and slightly burnt. Observer killed. Machine burnt.' With these victories, Voss had begun a tally that would approach but never surpass Richthofen's as leading ace, although by March 1917 Richthofen regarded his friend Voss as his 'vigorous competitor'.

Richthofen would not shoot down another F.E.2 until 20 December, when he downed 18 Sqn F.E.2b A5446 at 1345 hours over Moreuil. Instead, he found himself on the victorious end of several engagements with DH.2s. The first of these was on 11 December, when just south of Arras at 1145 hours Richthofen and Ltn d R Wortmann spotted 32 Sqn DH.2s escorting 23 Sqn F.E.2bs on a bombing sortie. Singling out DH.2 5986, flown by three-victory 'B' Flight Ltn B. P. G. Hunt, Richthofen gave chase and 'after a short curve fight I ruined the adversary's motor and forced him to land behind our lines near Mercatel.' Nine days later, on 20 December, Richthofen was leading five Albatros from Jasta 2 on a patrol at 3,000 metres near Monchy-au-Bois when at 1130 hours they tangled with 29 Sqn DH.2s out on offensive patrol. After the initial clash, the battle dissolved into a series of individual combats, and Richthofen entered a turning battle with DH.2 7927 flown by eight-victory ace Capt Arthur Knight. Twenty-one-year-old Knight had transferred from 24 Sqn the previous month, where as a lieutenant in October he had been the pilot Richthofen had chased in front of Boelcke and Böhme to cause their mid-air collision. Chased by Richthofen again, Knight evaded the German ace until they had descended to 1,500 metres, where Richthofen was attacked 'at closest range (plane length). I saw immediately that I had hit the enemy; first he went down in curves, then he dashed to the ground.' Richthofen followed Knight down to within 100 metres of the ground to verify his victory, and to secure the claim he noted in his combat report that 'this plane had only been attacked by me.' Knight, who had been killed either by aerial gunfire or the ensuing crash, became Richthofen's 13th victory.

On 21 December, Voss scored his third victory, a 7 Sqn B.E.2d that he shot down while artillery spotting near Miraumont at 1100 hours. On the 26th, Bohme and König shot down two more B.E.2s (both C-types), while Ltn d R Dieter Collin shot down his second, a 24 Sqn DH.2 near Morval. The final Jasta 2 victory for the year came one day later, when Richthofen led a patrol of five Albatrosses south of Arras and encountered 29 Sqn DH.2s, one of which was flown by then single-victory but future 57-victory and RFC luminary Flt Sgt James McCudden, who recalled that after seeing 'five HA' he attacked an Albatros that had latched onto the tail of a DH.2 flown by Lt Jennings.

This Albatros was flown by Richthofen, who summarily disengaged and reversed course to attack McCudden head-on. Although in his 1918 *Air Combat Operations Manual* Richthofen opined that head-on attacks against two-seaters (which, as will be seen, he thought McCudden was flying) were 'very dangerous', in late 1916 he was still refining the lessons learned from

Boelcke and had not compiled enough experience to conclude the tactical ineffectiveness of this method of attack. In January 1917 (by then flying the new Albatros D.III) he was still experimenting with head-on attacks, although against single-seaters, such as when he encountered 40 Sqn F.E.8s on the 23rd and attacked Lt E. L. Benbow from head-on, who dived away and escaped.

Much the same result occurred initially in the fight with McCudden, who wrote:

> This Hun at once came for me nose on, and we both fired simultaneously [his combat report stated 'from 100 yards'], but after firing about twenty shots [his combat report stated eight] my gun got a bad double feed, which I could not rectify at the time as I was now in the middle of five D.I Albatrosses, so I half-rolled.

However, in this instance Richthofen gave chase, so that when McCudden recovered and pulled level,

> 'cack, cack, cack, cack' came from just behind me, and on looking round I saw my old friend with the black and white streamers again. I immediately half-rolled again, but still the Hun stayed there.

The tenacious Richthofen pursued the fleeing McCudden in this manner until they were a mile over the lines in English territory, at which point hostile AA fire forced Richthofen to disengage at 800 feet and turn east for his lines. Finally free from pursuit, McCudden rectified his jammed gun and turned his DH.2 after the retreating Albatros, but 'by this time the Hun was much higher, and very soon joined his patrol, who were waiting for him at about 5,000 feet over Ransart.'

Mistakenly, Richthofen claimed he had chased 'a very courageously flying Vickers two-seater' (referring to the F.E.2b, a pusher that resembled a DH.2

Albatros D.III prototype at Johannisthal, 1916. As is typical with Albatros prototypes, the machine is unarmed and without serial number. The new sesquiplane design and resultant interplane struts gave the machine a racier appearance, yet introduced structural problems that led to fatal accidents, grounding, and modification. Although never completely rectified, by spring 1917 the D.III was back in the air and inflicting serious casualties upon the RFC.

but which was a larger two-seater) that 'crashed to the ground on the enemy side'. Clearly, McCudden had not crashed. In the frantic pace of their spinning combat it is easy to understand how Richthofen misidentified his adversary's machine, and air batteries 13 and 47 were listed as corroborating witnesses to the 'victory' in Richthofen's combat report. However, although McCudden's DH.2 had been 'chased absolutely out of the sky from 10,000 feet to 800 feet', Richthofen's 15th credited victory and his last for 1916 was not an actual victory at all.

CONCLUSION

Aerial combat slackened considerably as 1917 arrived and winter gripped Europe. Although the Albatros D.I and D.II flew and fought when the weather allowed, their front-line inventory began fading with the arrival of their replacement, the Albatros D.III. Still, they had left their mark. After their arrival in mid-September 1916, Major-General Hugh Trenchard, the Officer Commanding the Royal Flying Corps in France, reported: 'I have come to the conclusion that the Germans have brought another squadron or squadrons of fighting machines to this neighbourhood and also more artillery machines.' Although this early attention was warranted, based on observed performance superiority, new tactics, and the fighting aggression of the new German fighters, the number of aeroplanes had not been enough to arrest the aggressive strategy of the RFC. Trenchard remained confident:

> the anti-aircraft guns have only reported 14 hostile machines as having crossed the line in the 4th Army area in the last week ... whereas something like 2,000 to 3,000 of our machines crossed the lines during the week.

Yet with the D.I, D.II, and new Jagdstaffeln causing increasing casualties, Commander-in-Chief of the British Expeditionary Force Sir Douglas Haig recognized approaching hardships. On 30 September, just two weeks after the Albatros D.Is first arrived at Jasta 2, he wrote to the War Office that

Albatros company logo. Applied to the top rear areas of both sides of the rudder, this logo usually faced ('flew toward') the spinner, although there were occasional exceptions. (Drawn by and courtesy of Michael Backus)

'the enemy has made extraordinary efforts to increase the number, and develop the speed and power, of his fighting machines' – a clear reference to the D.I and D.II.

> He has unfortunately succeeded in doing so and it is necessary to realize clearly, and at once, that we shall undoubtedly lose our superiority in the air if I am not provided at an early date with the improved means of retaining it.

Even more bluntly, he wrote:

> The result of the advent of the enemy's improved machines [Albatros D.I, D.II] has been a marked increase in the casualties suffered by the Royal Flying Corps, and though I do not anticipate losing our present predominance in the air for the next three or four months, the situation after that threatens to be very serious unless adequate steps to deal with it are taken at once.

By then Albatros had already produced the prototype of the D.II's successor, the D.III. Influenced by the French Nieuport's sesquiplane design, the D.III featured reduced chord lower wings of single-spar construction, with the interplane struts joining these wings in the classic 'V' that all subsequent Albatros models retained. The D.III arrived at the Front *en masse* in early 1917, and once the weather broke the RFC still did not possess a fighter that could arrest the Albatros's onslaught against their reconnaissance machines. Just as Haig had fretted, that spring they suffered appalling casualties in a desperate period known as 'Bloody April'.

However, the D.III's success bore a high price. The new sesquiplane design led to structural flaws that caused in-flight wing failures, resulting in the

Oeffag company logo, applied to both sides of the fuselage near the front engine cowls.

deaths of several pilots, and Idflieg grounded the aeroplane until the lower wings of the remaining machines were strengthened or replaced. Even after their return to service three weeks later, German pilots knew not to prosecute a dive too aggressively lest they invite structural catastrophe. Despite these troubles and limitations, they extracted a serious toll on the enemy through the spring of 1917, but as the year progressed they faced an increasing number of new enemy fighter types, including the Sopwith Pup, Sopwith Triplane, SPAD VII, and SE 5a. Tactically the Albatros D.III still gave a good account of itself, but, strategically, the superiority pendulum had begun its swing back toward the RFC.

BIBLIOGRAPHY

Connors, J. F., *Albatros Fighters in Action*, Squadron/Signal Publications (1981)

Fant, D. V., 'Many Battles and Many a Bold Adventure', *Over the Front*, vol. 5, no. 1 (Spring 1990), pp. 35–52

Franks, N., *Jagdstaffel Boelcke*, Grub Street (2004)

Gardner, B., *WW1 Aircraft Propellers, Volume Three*, Circadian (UK) Ltd (2008)

Gray, B. J., 'The Anatomy of an Aeroplane', *Cross & Cockade International*, vol. 20, no. 1, (1989), pp. 1–25

Grosz, P. M., *Albatros D.I/D.II*, Windsock Datafile 100, Albatross Publications (2003)

Grosz, P. M., *Fokker Fighters D.I-D.IV*, Windsock Classics of WW1 Aviation 2, Albatross Publications (1999)

Grosz, P. M., Haddow, G., and Schiemer, P., *Austro-Hungarian Army Aircraft of World War One*, Flying Machine Press (1993)

Guttman, J., *The Origin of the Fighter Aircraft*, Westholme Publishing (2009)

Guttman, J., *Pusher Aces of World War 1*, Osprey Publishing (2009)

Hawker, T. M., *Hawker VC*, Mitre Press (1965)

Höfling, R., *Albatros D-II: Germany's Legendary World War I Fighter*, Schiffer Books (2002)

Kilduff, P., *The Red Baron*, Doubleday (1969)

Kilduff, P., *Red Baron: The Life and Death of an Ace*, David & Charles Ltd (2007)

Leaman, P., *Fokker Aircraft of World War One*, Crowood Press Ltd (2001)

Lewis, G. H., *Wings Over the Somme 1916–1918*, William Kimber & Co. Ltd (1976)

McCudden, J., *Flying Fury: Five Years in the Royal Flying Corps*, Greenhill (2000)

Mikesh, R. C., *Albatros D.Va, German Fighter of World War I*, Smithsonian Institution Press (1980)

Miller, J. F., 'Eight Minutes Near Bapaume', *Over the Front*, vol. 21, no. 2 (Summer 2006), pp. 120–138

Miller, J. F., *Manfred von Richthofen: The Aircraft, Myths and Accomplishments of 'The Red Baron'*, Air Power Editions (2009)

O'Connor, M., *Air Aces of the Austro-Hungarian Empire 1914–1918*, Flying Machine Press (1986)

Revell, A., *British Single-Seater Fighter Squadrons on the Western Front in World War I*, Schiffer Books (2006)

Steel, N., and Hart, P., *Tumult in the Clouds*, Coronet Books (1997)

Tesar, P., *Albatros D.II & D.III Oeffag*, JaPo (1998)

Van Wyngarden, G., *Albatros Aces of World War 1, Part 2*, Osprey Publishing (2007)

Van Wyngarden, G., *Early German Aces of World War 1*, Osprey Publishing (2006)

Van Wyngarden, G., *Jagdstaffel 2 'Boelcke': Von Richthofen's Mentor*, Osprey Publishing (2007)

Williams, A. G., and Gustin E., *Flying Guns of World War I*, Crowood Press Ltd (2003)

INDEX

References to illustrations are shown in **bold**